CONCE

BEFORE THE ALTAR

A HUNDRED VISITS
To Jesus
in the Blessed Sacrament

Kathleen,

I wish you a very Merry Christmas!
and a wonderful year 2014!
I hope you like this beautiful
meditations about the Blessed
Sacrament of the Eucharistic.
Love,
Adriana.

Before the Altar

By: Concepcion Cabrera De Armida
(Conchita)

ISBN#189128035X

Publisher:
  CMJ Marian Publishers & Distribution
  Post Office Box 661
  Oak Lawn, IL 60454

  www.cmjbooks.com
  Phone 708-636-2995

Manufactured in the United States of America with permission.

Graphics: New Creation Graphics
           635 Hickory Court
           Davis, IL 61019

CMJ
Marian Publishers
Soul Assurance Prayer Plan

Revised by
Ronda De Sola Chervin

With an introduction by
Msgr. Juan Esquerda Bifet

NIHIL OBSTAT
F. Thomas Berhg, O.S.B.
Censor Deputatus
Aug. 1913

Twenty five editions
in Spanish, French, Italian
and English

TABLE OF CONTENTS

FOREWORD

I was twelve years old, at the Minor Seminary of the Missionaries of the Holy Spirit (or Escuela Apostolica), when I first heard of Concepción Cabrera de Armida. Many of the priests who came to visit us had known her and used to speak of "Conchita" with great affection. In 1962 I participated at Conchita's centennial birthday celebration. It was there, in Mexico City, that I first met some of her children and other people who had lived with her.

As the years have passed, I have come to know her native city, the churches she used to visit, the "haciendas" where she spent her childhood and the roads and mountains where she prayed, engulfed in the immensity of God. By now I have read most of her works. All of this has helped me to better understand Conchita, her literary style and the content of her writings.

I have written these pages thinking of you, dear reader, as you draw near to this "jewel of spiritual literature," as Msgr. John Esquerda Bifet has called it in his introduction; about you who because of your culture are unlike the author, and who live in a different historical and theological moment from the moment when this work was born. I hope that these lines might help you know a little about the Author of Before the Altar: her family background, her personality, her language, her spiritual quest, her loves.

Conchita was born in 1862 in the city of San Luis Potosí, a colonial city in the center of the Mexican Republic. Her parents were outstanding Christians, combining devotion and charity, love of God and love of neighbor in their home.

Conchita lived long periods of time on the haciendas. She remembers how close contact with nature would elevate her soul to God. The churches of her native city were also the scene of many intimate moments of prayer. There, as was the custom of the time, Conchita attended Holy Mass many times and listened to long and elaborate sermons, full of biblical and patristic quotations, and edifying examples taken from the lives of the saints. All this without a doubt enhanced what she had heard and read in the book Año Cristiano (The Christian Year). Little by little in her mind and in her heart, "a treasure" began to form of known facts and of affective responses which she later expressed in a personal manner in her writing.

Her prayer life, both formal and spontaneous, was enriched in a special way by the teaching she received, first at the College of the Sacred Heart and then with the aid of the Spiritual Exercises of Saint Ignatius, in which meditation on the mysteries of the life of Christ, the use of the imagination, and interior reconstruction of the various scriptural passages began to leave a profound imprint on her heart.

Interwoven in her experience one finds housework and the life of prayer; contact with God and service to one's neighbor; love of the Eucharist and love of her husband and children; social life and religious experience; all of this forming a simple and vital unity which will be clearly seen in her writings.

By the time Conchita wrote *Before the Altar* between 1903 and 1904, she had already received many prayer graces mentioned by Saint John of the Cross and Saint Teresa of Avila (quiet prayer,

prayer of the heart, affective prayer, union of wills, etc.). Before the Altar is born of the pen of a mystic: someone for whom God is her center; her only love, the point of reference from which she lives. The passion to speak of the beloved becomes a necessity. Possessor of proficient literary gifts, having a refined feminine sensitivity, and using a typically Mexican vocabulary, she easily knows how to communicate that which she bears within, imbuing her writings with a warmth which easily reaches the heart of the reader.

As Dr. Chervin says in her "preface," *Before the Altar* was not initially written for the general public. The Venerable Servant of God, Félix de Jesús Rougier M.Sp.S., realizing the blessings that the work would bring to so many people that long for God, promoted the first editions of *Before the Altar* in French, English, Italian and German and their distribution in Europe.

When Conchita left this world, forty-six of her works of different lengths had been published. In total she wrote 158 volumes, the most important one being her Spiritual Diary. Fr. Juan Gutiérrez González M.Sp.S. has recently published the most important parts of this diary in Spanish under the title "Concepcion Cabrera de Armida, Cruz de Jesus (Cross of Jesus)," Vol IX. We hope to have this work translated into English in the near future.

In the meantime the reader can become familiar with the life and spirituality of the Venerable Servant of God in the book entitled: *Conchita: A Mother's Spiritual Diary*, by M. M. Philipon, O.P., Alba House, 2nd Edition, 2000.

After her having lived so close to God, filled with good works, and having been considered saintly at her death, Conchita's beatification process was begun in Mexico City in 1956. Once all the necessary documents had been collected and all the witnesses had testified, everything was sent to Rome in 1959. Then followed a very thorough study and long process. Finally, her life, her virtues and her fame of hollyness were analyzed by the consulting theologians of the Cause for the Saints on March 2, 1999 and by a group of cardinals and bishops on October 19 of the same year. His Holiness Pope John Paul II conferred the title of Venerable to Concepcion Cabrera de Armida on December 21, 1999.

I invite the readers of *Before the Altar* to turn their gaze upon this woman, wife and mother and invoke God that through her intercession, He might pour out many graces upon us. May God deign to grant us the miracle which the Church requests in order to be able to officially declare Conchita, first Blessed and then a Saint.

I pray to the Holy Spirit that contact with this book brings the reader to love Christ as much as Conchita loved Him.

Fr. Domenico Di Raimondo, M.Sp.S.
Postulator General

INTRODUCTION
by Msgr. Juan Esquerda Bifet

We find ourselves in the presence of a book which because of its many editions might be called a classic within the spirituality. Within its several chapters appear the most revealing fragments of the spiritual doctrine of Concepción Cabrera de Armida, «Conchita», whose whole self is molded in the encounter with Jesus present in the Holy Eucharist. The reader may perhaps recognize some portions of that life spent for love of Jesus Christ and of his Church. The basic biographical data denote a life full of the «perfect joy» of sharing the very life of the Lord.[1]

This book has not been written to «know about» Christ, i.e., to impart knowledge, but to enable the reader to live the experience of the encounter with Christ, in a relaxed and leisurely manner. Whoever might wish to summarize the ideas of this book without having lived them experientially in the presence of Jesus in the Blessed Eucharist, will find only the linguistic

---

[1] For Biographical data see Fr. Philipon's Chronology; *Conchita: A Mother's Spiritual Diary*, English Edition, Alba House, New York, 1978, pp. 202-203.

expressions of an era. It is a contemplative, vocational and missionary booklet. Many have met Christ and have taken permanent hold of Him, thanks to this pearl of spiritual literature. They are «generous souls», who have followed the Lord «without hesitation».

The book has tremendous content matter: the whole of the Christian message related to the spiritual life. It easily lends itself to dialogue because it causes all the resources of the heart to be moved in order to elicit a response which will be one of total surrender without reserve. All of the evangelical themes appear before Christ in the Blessed Eucharist, present, immolated and communicated. For the mystery of his Incarnation, Redemption are the root of all affirmations.

The reader may readily see without the need of a great deal of explanation that it is comprised of dialogues with Jesus in the Eucharist. The believer expresses his/her desires to the Lord and then waits for a response from the Lord. With a little attention, the reader will realize that it means entering into the gospel and living it from the inside, from one heart to another, i.e., from heart to heart, because the gospel continues to take place when it is read in this manner.

Those dialogues tend to become a living gospel, a «crux viva» (a living cross) as Conchita would say. They are attainable themes like the doctrine of the saints and of good spiritual writings (which she frequently quotes), beginning with a living experience of God which serves as an invitation that each might have his/her own, ever irrepeatable experience. The language is typically Christian and as such, somewhat at the periphery of the other subjective and consumeristic sectors of our secular environment. At its center, and beyond the circumstantial expressions, which can always be improved upon, one finds the language of love, for love has but one rule: a totality of surrender through a totality of self-renunciation. «The Cross sanctifies, and I want to be holy». Such is the Cross of the Paschal Mystery.

We have said that all the Christian issues begin to emerge having one's dialogue with Jesus in the Eucharist as their point of origin. In effect, if the Eucharistic mystery is presence, sacrifice and communion, the believer feels himself or herself called to a dialogue which becomes an intimate following, espousal or friendship. We find here, then, the themes of vocation, of contemplation, of perfection and of mission.

There is an internal dynamic which is easily achieved by anyone who does not place limits on its love; the believer, in the presence of Christ in the Eucharist, feels himself/herself loved, accompanied, and enabled to love. From this is borne:

    — *a profound self-knowledge, without fear of love,*
    — *a limitless confidence in the love of God,*
    — *a decision to love Him in the most perfect manner possible.*

But all this is «grace», gift and initiative on God's part. That is why Christian issues are «learned» only by praying, from one heart to the other before the Tabernacle.

The process of the Spiritual life which appears in these Eucharistic dialogues is very simple:

    — *That only Jesus reign in one's heart («You alone are and shall ever be my only love»).*
    — *Emptying it of all that might not be Him («I shall empty myself that You may appear»).*
    — *With the deep desire of saving souls for Him («millions of souls to consecrate them to You», «a thirst for souls», «this is the cry of my heart»).*

As one can see, it means totally emptying oneself, in order to possess only Jesus: «The poorer I am, the more dear shall I be to your Heart». And then one shall find his/her own name written in the Heart of God.

It is true that today there is less emphasis on that personal dialogue with Christ. At times people prefer just to get together to discuss current issues and to resolve them as «best» as possible. I feel that we leave many people defenseless in the face of today's reality because we do not help them to progress in the living dialogue with Christ, who is the source of all true commitment to charity and to mission. The dialogues with Jesus in the Blessed Sacrament, written by Conchita, teach one to be with the Lord in a relaxed manner, experiencing a unique oneness with a really beloved person. One always finds time for someone one loves, and the person who loves Our Lord also finds time to listen to his laments over our lack of love. Reparation is a matter of tenderness between people who love one another.

One also sees in each of the dialogues and topics an action of the Holy Spirit, the Great unknown and forgotten One, Who guides the believer through a process of emptying of self, that is, of all that is not of love, in order that one might be filled with Christ and

like Him and with Him might become a gift to the
Father and to one's fellow women and men. In reality,
the celebration of the Eucharist and Eucharistic adoration are a privileged moment of the communication of
the Spirit, Who in some manner creates in each believer
a specie of «reproduction» of the Incarnation, «a new
Pentecost», a «most beloved spouse of the Holy Spirit».

The subject of the Cross, in light of the dialogue
with Christ, no longer appears with the coldness of a
«thing» or of a suffering from which one flees, but is in
fact a sharing in the very fortune or «cup» of the
Spouse, where one offers to be, like Him and with Him,
a «living Cross», because the Cross is «Jesus, Himself
transformed into it». Finally it means the making of
one's own life a sacrificial donation: «I am happy with
these splinters from the Cross, for the measure of
renunciation is love». To be a «victim» with Jesus
means allowing Him to live in one's own heart. «May
your Cross be my Cross».

The Eucharistic dialogue is made in a climate of
confidence, friendly relationship, intimate union,
mutual gift, transformation, and imitation. The
demands are many, but they are merely those that
derive from a love relationship. The love of Christ is
then discovered with a new perspective:

— *He loves because He is good, not for any merit of our own,*
— *«with a greater desire of giving us his graces than we have of receiving them»,*
— *sustaining in us full confidence:«You did not need me . . . You willed to need my love».*

And what is the theme of the contemplation? It has the sense of a simple look or of a search that leaves the sensation of absence: «Where are you that my longing soul does not find you?» That search is then an encounter, but beginning with the dialogue, one must learn that «silence» that is not an emptiness, but is full of a «presence» which is discovered beyond that which appears to be absence. «Jesus is found in that silence which surrounds his tabernacles», far beyond that which we are able to imagine, say, feel. Life becomes a search and an encounter: «I seek you with every beat of my heart». «Let us never forget one another . . .» «I contemplating your expressions of love, and you having compassion on my miseries». «My life is encompassed from God to God . . .» «I came from Him and I go to Him; but when?» We must allow Jesus to continue to amaze us.

There, you have, then, the entirety of the spiritual life: the Lord speaks to declare his love for us, we listen determined to love Him above all and to cause Him to be loved by all. No one can take our place in that dialogue, because each one of us has his name written in that Heart. Then all one's life becomes deeply related to Christ («He is found at my side»), spent in a love that encompasses the total self («I die without Him Who is my life»). Jesus, our Spouse, does not place limits on his love: «My child, give me your heart». That is how we learn to «see as He saw».

The reality that we must face may seem difficult at face value, but all life becomes beautiful, because Jesus is the Way: «my way . . . is Jesus Himself; that is why I enter into Him without hesitation, despite the splinters». The joy above all joys shall be to live from the Cross, which Christ shall communicate to us, to be a share in the chalice of his wedding feast, so that we might also share with Him his evangelizing fruitfulness, «from one end of the world to the other».

Every topic that appears in the dialogues is a gospel phrase or fact, presented and motivated, with the intention that it be enfleshed by us, and as it is meant to be «meditated in one's heart» (Luke 2:51), Mary is always presented as Mother, model and intercessor. Mary also lived «crucified . . . in order to resemble Jesus more closely». For this reason we want to live the topics described in the dialogues with Mary and as Mary did: «Jesus, who belonged to Mary and also belongs to me», to love Jesus «like you loved Him», «with the very beating of your heart», with a «martyr's love», because «your heart never stopped praying», «between Him and I, you stand». «O Mary, you who truly loved your Jesus with an unsurpassable, inseparable, singular and insatiable love, grant us your heart so that with it we might love Him Who is love».

Jesus waits for us in the Eucharist to take upon Himself, from this standpoint, our reality of limitation and poverty. Each dialogue from "Before the Altar," leaves us alone with the Lord. Realizing in the presence of the Eucharist, our own limited reality, we find ourselves with the surprise that Jesus waits for us precisely in that situation or event in order to make Himself one with us, i.e., to form solidarity with us. The text of the dialogue leaves room for Jesus Himself to speak to each one in an irrepeatable manner, from one heart to another.

Beginning with this evangelical and eucharistic experience, we learn that life becomes a permanent encounter with Christ. We find Him in his Word, in his Eucharist, in our fellow women and men, in events, in our solitude, in our work, ever moving *toward that final encounter beyond. Meanwhile, prayer continues to be a simple gazing and a confident dialogue: «Lord, teach me what You want me to say to You». We set out upon the life of surrender each day, with the decision to live related to Christ in order to meet Him and love Him in all our brothers and sisters. Then life is truly beautiful because it is lived for Him.*

Juan Esquerda Bifet

PREFACE
by Ronda De Sola Chervin

Some five years ago Rev. Eugenio Cardenas, of the Missionaries of the Holy Spirit, gave me a copy of *Before the Altar* to read for meditation. As I am sure is the case with many other North American readers, even though I found the thoughts beautiful and inspiring, I was often distracted by the use in the translation of many English words from bygone eras.

For this reason I was delighted when I was asked if I would be willing to assist the Missionaries and the Sisters of the Cross by going through the English text of 1913 and rendering a new edition with a more American use of words.

Once I began this happy work, pursued out of love for the grace-filled words of my beloved Conchita, I had to admit that it was not just the oldfashioned words of the former translation that made the text difficult to read in our times, but even more importantly the intensity of a spirituality so different from contemporary ideas that it could seem at times repellent even to eager readers such as myself.

Challenged to the limit by certain themes characteristic of Conchita's spirituality of the Cross, the modern reader wants to overcome his or her reluctance to go quite that far by shrugging off the more demanding passages as written for a chosen few, not universal, and, therefore, certainly not something I must take seriously.

As I worked on my rendition of *Before the Altar* I gradually received the grace to see that the call is universally given. Very few will hear this call, however, because many of us have not reached a level of spiritual growth where such words can be understood.

In conversing about this problem with Fr. Domenico Di Raimondo, M.Sp.S., I found that certain insights could help me be more open to the message from Jesus Conchita wished so much to convey through her meditations for Eucharistic Adoration.

First of all Fr. Domenico pointed out that originally the prayers were composed for the use of Fr. Felix, the founder of the Missionaries of the Holy Spirit, a man of the highest spiritual maturity, certainly not for beginners.

Another important consideration is that the book was written for those who had already understood that it was not suffering for its own sake that was being exalted, but suffering for love, in love.

Let us take one example. Throughout *Before the Altar* we are taught to accept as part of our cross in life being treated badly by others. Not only must we accept it, we must beg in prayer to be treated with indifference and ingratitude... forgotten and forsaken. On pondering this teaching I came to realize how liberating it could be. Consider how much energy most of us expend in seeking human approval. The anxious watching of the faces of others to see if they value us as much as we wish them to, deprives us in almost all encounters with others of peace and dignity. In a subtle way, that inordinate desire for affirmation from friends and associates keeps us from seeking the face of Jesus whose loving approval of our actions can alone give us steady joy.

Or consider the many lines in the book about renouncing one's own judgments and opinions. Conchita's admonition does not refer to judgements and ideas that concern the perennial truths of our Catholic faith but, rather, the level of ideas and opinions that concern relative ways of doing things which nevertheless, out of pride, take on a false sense of importance such as ideas about events, personalities, remedies.

Holding on to our own ideas about such matters can become a matter of ego. It creates division. A holy person holds firm to absolute truth and otherwise listens with interest to others, trying to learn rather than trying to be a universal expert.

By the middle of my work I began to realize that even if I was far from the level of spirituality of many of the members of the orders founded by Conchita and Fr. Felix, that I needed to humbly listen to the inspirations of the Holy Spirit contained in this advanced book of prayer. Just as beginners in music are urged not only to listen to their own deficient playing but to great symphonies played by instrumentalists far beyond their own level, so it is important that we read not only contemporary books of spirituality for everyday living, or our own journal writings no matter how personal and sincere, but also the sentiments of the saints even though we are far from the total self-surrender their words express. I also began to appreciate the marvelous poetic imagery that grows from meditation to meditation.

As, myself, a writer of many books in the area of lay spirituality such as *Treasury of Women Saints*, *Prayers of the Women Mystics*, *Woman to Woman* (with Terri Vorndran Nichols), *Spiritual Friendship: The Darkness and the Light*, I was also impressed by how much women entering into spiritual friendships with lay-men, priests and brothers could benefit from meditating together on *Before the Altar* as a means of participating in the fire of sacrificial love for Christ that purified the union of souls of Conchita and Fr. Felix.

May I end my short preface to the new text of *Before the Altar* with this prayer:

May all who read this book composed by Conchita in the spirit of total self-surrender to her beloved Jesus receive the grace to be similarly transformed from ardor to holiness, especially me.

Ronda De Sola Chervin

1. YOU ALONE

Jesus, God and Spouse of my soul! You alone, you alone . . . when shall I finally understand it?

I shall always find you available, O my Jesus, to listen to me, day and night, always!

If I cling to human affection I shall find nothing but disenchantment and disappointment!

Thank you, O my good Jesus, thank you. In your mercy tear me away from all that is not yourself.

Send me experiences of deception, misfortune; let me be treated with indifference and ingratitude; let me be forgotten and forsaken, in your mercy, so that all that is earthly may be removed from my heart. Do this for the good of my soul which is so inclined to attach itself to creatures and which, nevertheless, desires only to belong to you, my Jesus.

May all that is evil in my heart be taken far away from me, O my adorable Jesus! May the bad seeds which lie within my heart perish, and may the first fruits of my sufferings be always for you alone.

May I do all the good I possibly can, and yet may no one ever be grateful to me for it.

Slaves are made use of, and then they are forgotten; oh, how I envy them!

O my Jesus! What I want, however much pain it may bring me, is to render service to others and to be repaid with ingratitude in exchange for my kindness.

It is a glorious ideal, and I am unworthy to attain it, nevertheless I will pursue it; whatever be the cost!

In this way, with my soul detached from creatures, and purified by sacrifice and voluntary humiliations, I shall fly to you, my Jesus, and you alone shall be my reward and my all.

You alone! What sweet echoes do these words create in my innermost being! You alone; my God . . . my only one, and my all!

You alone, from now on, shall be the one to whom I confide my loves and my sufferings. You alone shall dwell in my soul . . . You alone shall be my hope and my heaven on earth.

You alone, my good Master, shall console me in my sorrows, dry my tears, and be my companion at the hour of my death, when all others shall forsake me. And last of all, your picture, this adored image on the cross which I have kissed during life shall be the silent witness of my total destruction in the grave.

This is why you alone, O my Jesus. You alone shall ever be my only love.

Amen.

2. IT IS GETTING LATE

O yes, Jesus, my Life! The end of my day is approaching and I wish to keep quite close to you, for the cold chills me if I withdraw from you ever so little. In order to be happy and at peace, I need the gentle warmth of your heart, of your words, and of your glance.

Night is coming on, O Jesus hidden within the Host; my hands are empty of virtues, and I need your merits and your cross to fill them. But where shall I find all these graces? Where shall I turn to look for these treasures, if not to the foot of the beloved altar where you dwell, O my adorable Master?

I have wasted the better part of my life in vanities, in fantasies, in vain pleasures, and in foolish illusions.

My days have passed while I was leading an earthly life, without once raising my eyes to Heaven, without remembering the purity of intention which I ought always to have had.

There are immense areas of neglect in my life: I have not always done my duty to my neighbor, or to the members of my family, nor have I fulfilled the most holy obligations of religion.

Instead of seeking God, I have sought myself. I have desired comforts, I have been vainglorious and obstinate in defending my own opinion. I have taken pleasure in worldly friendships, and have sought my own gratification even in my special prayertime alone with you!

How often have I yielded to a desire to have others approve of me, to being too easily hurt, to culpable weaknesses!

How much self-indulgence, what excuses, what idleness, pleasure seeking, and sluggishness in the service of God; what imprudence, what vainglory, touchiness, cowardice and uncharitableness! O my Jesus, it makes me tremble when I consider that it is the end of the day, that night is coming on, and that my heart, alas, remains full of vices, stains and iniquities!

Have not envy, jealousy, and pride invaded even my life in religion, which should have been a life of sanctity; an angelic life, and one of self-immolation?

Where are the humility, the patience, the obedience, the gentleness, the costly victories;

where the sacrifice, which was to be the very essence of my life in this community?

Where are to be found that unlimited charity, that contempt of myself, that ardent desire of self-immolation, that thirst for suffering, that hunger for solitude, that oblivion, that detachment from those I love best . . . in all of which I should have placed my happiness?

Do I really wish to be the lowliest among my brethren? Do I feel it a joy to be poor and miserable for love of you?

Alas! It is not so, O my Jesus! And this is why I suffer, because my hands are empty, and the Bridegroom will soon be here. And I shall have neither the oil of virtues nor the ardent flame of love, to offer him!

3. COMPLAINTS

Why, O Jesus!, my Own, my Life, my All, do you hide yourself from me? Why cannot my soul, which adores you, find you? Why, Jesus here present with me, do you seem to be indifferent to my ardent love? Why do you shrink from my caresses and let my tears flow without any consolation? Why this disdain, O my Love, for a soul which lives only on your Life, your doctrine, your words, and which desires no other music but the sweet sound of your voice?

Why do those Divine eyes which enchant me shun my gaze and turn away from me?

Why does that Heart, whose fiery flames I have felt so often, which has beaten against my heart, which has made mine leap for joy a thousand times, why does it appear today to be unconscious of my tears and of my sufferings?

Why, Life of my life, Source of my being? Light of my darkness, Heaven of my soul, why do you shun and apparently forget me, while my heart is consumed with desire to possess you?

Why, at the moment of my receiving you, O Sacred Host, do you, who are my Life, my Love and my Action, palpitate in my soul, while I am dying, alas, in inactivity, indifference, impotence, and weakness?

Why is it that, living as I do beneath the burning rays of my Eucharistic Sun, everything around me is ice, indifference and pain?

Why, Love of my loves, my Heaven, my Life, Heart of my soul, why leave my soul to be immersed and drowning in an ocean of suffering?

Why, O my Jesus, do you not listen to me? Why do you seem insensitive to the tears which fall burning at your feet?

Why are you indifferent to my loving glances, to my embraces? Why O my Jesus? Why?

Is it for my sins or for those of others?

Is it to punish me? Is it out of love and to purify me? O my Beloved, chosen among a thousand, do not forsake me: have pity on me, for it is death to me to be without him who is my Life!

My days are nights, my nights a purgatory, my mind a hell . . . The hours are a continual martyrdom without him who is my Light, my very breath, my heart and my Heaven!

O Jesus, Jesus, what shall I do to find you? Ah, I know! Not to find myself, who am the cause of my own unhappiness. I must disappear, diminish, descend, and be reduced to nothing, in order that you must grow, and reign, occupy in my heart the place which I have prepared for you!

Yes, that is what I am going to do, O Jesus here present with me in the Holy Eucharist! Disappear, that you must appear; make a void in my soul, so that you must fill it up, reduce me to nothing so that you must be All in the heart of your poor child.

Amen.

4. YOU SHALL ALWAYS BE WITH ME

O Jesus! Love of my soul, you shall always remain with me, you, even if I should lose all else: my father, and my mother, my family, my director, my friends, my superiors and my brethren in religion . . . Yes, you shall remain, for you do not die, you change not and the fire of your Heart is as ardent as ever!

What matters to me therefore, the long distance which separates me from those I love, if my Love, if he who keeps hidden in his Heart all the tenderness of the earth, is to be found at my side?

In saying goodbye to my father and my mother, I have come near you, O Jesus, who are truly Father and a thousand times mother.

At the remembrance of my brothers, my friends and all those whom I have left in the world, I think of you, and I feel the most intimate recesses of my soul overwhelmed by your love.

I remember those who have gone before me into Eternity, and my eyes are turned towards you, O Savior of my soul, because it is there that I come across them. It is there that they wait for me, bathed in the brightness of your pure and holy light.

Everything shall pass away, O Master of my life! The days and nights, the months and the years, the light and the darkness, the creatures that surround me; but you will never pass away. You, my Master, my Spouse, and my only Love. You will remain with me forever! On earth, friendships grow cold, human beings change, attachments become weakened, love itself vanishes and dies; but your affection, your tenderness and your love do not change, do not pass away but remain forever!

That is why I place all my happiness in possessing you, in having you to be mine; in adoring you with all the powers of my soul; in loving you passionately, madly, with all the tenderness of all loving hearts; with all the heartbeats of pure souls.

I should like to have a store of love to love you with; of caresses to caress you with; to dispose of millions of souls, o Jesus, that I might consecrate them to you!

What matters if everything earthly fails me, and if I lose friends, riches and even life itself, if you remain with me, you, who are the Life of lives, O my adorable Jesus? . . .

What happiness for me to have found heaven on earth! To have met Jesus, the Son of Mary, ever eager to press me to his Heart; and what joy, O Jesus, to think that you never change, that you remain unceasingly with us, that your friendship is ever the same, and that you are ever living! Jesus Christ the same yesterday, today and forever.

What an unutterable consolation to keep one's eyes fixed on your Divine Heart, so good, so loving; and to hear you saying in my inmost soul: My child, give me your heart.

5. LOOK, JESUS, HOW POOR I AM

Yes, Jesus, I am poor and have that voluntary poverty which rejoices in possessing nothing and in returning everything to you.

I long for actual poverty, and I am dying of love for this virtue, because I love you and wish to be like you, O Jesus of my soul!

But I wish to be poor also in many other things, and it is this grace I have come to ask of you with all my heart today.

I wish to be poor in honor and in all human praise.

I wish to possess poverty of spirit, and spiritual bereavement, with a complete emptiness of self, O my adorable Jesus!

I wish to be poor in human esteem and friendship.

I wish to come to the point of being happy to be abandoned, forgotten, treated indifferently and contemptuously by those I love most.

I wish to rejoice, O my God, in the thought that no one thinks of me, or has compassion on me: Do not weep for me did you not say, my Jesus? And I, too, wish to learn to suffer alone, to keep intact in my soul the mystery of the Cross.

I wish to be poor in consolation and to make my riches consist in poverty, so that the poorer I am, the more I shall excite your generosity and soften your Heart.

The more miserable and unhappy I shall be, the better right I shall have to your favors and graces.

O my God! I wish not to be, not to have . . . I wish to be less. I wish to be reduced to nothing for the love of you.

I wish to be poor in the friendship of creatures. Furthermore, O my Eucharistic Jesus, I wish to leave empty the place I occupy in other hearts, that you yourself may occupy it.

O, what a precious exchange, what a truly heavenly thing; you, reigning in the souls of others, and I, like a slave, at everybody's feet in the dust.

O Jesus, Light of my Life! Will you grant me this grace, for the love of your heavenly Father!

My wealth shall be my misfortune. I shall be happy in my littleness, in my inactivity, and in my nothingness.

O poverty of the soul, glorious and well beloved poverty, come to my arms, come to my heart!

But, my Jesus, I beg of you to listen to me. I have no love with which to love you, I have no sufferings to offer you: come to my assistance, O my only Good!

Give me the treasures of the cross which are the same as those of Heaven! I wish for thorns, and those beloved sufferings which are your delight and mine. I wish for all that the world abhors, for that is what you have taught me to love.

O my King, to whom I give up all that I possess, give me grace to deprive myself voluntarily of all that is pleasing to nature, and at the same time to abandon myself entirely into your hands!

Amen.

6. MY WAY

How beautiful it is! because it is Jesus himself: and therefore I travel through it without stumbling, even when treading on thorns.

I notice every day new fruits to be gathered on this holy Way of the Cross, and in order to do so I must renounce my own judgment and lacerate my heart for love of Jesus. But no matter. There lies the precious and enviable way. Happy shall I be if I keep on it to the end!

Is it not true, my Jesus, that it is you who are this enchanting Way?

— Yes, my son, I am this way of suffering, which you must enter upon without delay.

The real interior life is the life that is lived in me, in imitating me, ever choosing the path of suffering with a soul in love with the cross. This is the solid, spiritual way, along the path to Calvary, which you must follow.

Through me lies the only possible way to perfection, and it is only in following me that the soul can be transformed into an agreeable victim, rendered divine by its union with me.

Come to my arms, my beloved son, for I am the Life; come and drink it in and at the same time drink in the Truth which leads to heaven.

I am a Way, but a Way of virtues, a way of blood . . . a Way of sorrows over which love alone can travel! . . . a Way so far reaching that its limits can only be discerned by eyes of the greatest purity.

Few souls enter fully into this way of which I have spoken, saying I am the Way, but you must pass over every part of it. It is full of obstacles and dangers, but those who follow it find also heavenly joys. Do you know why?

Because love alone can cross it, the love which is born and has grown up in the love of the Cross.

— Ah, that is the love that I desire, my Jesus, that love so pure which has sprung up from the midst of trials. O, how beautiful is that love, adorned with the colors of the crucified Savior of my soul! Give me that love, my Jesus, give it to me so that I may console you.

I wish to love you in suffering, O Jesus! and that my consolation may consist in not receiving consolation!

Give me that love of Calvary, that love which is immeasurable, as it reaches to heaven!

The cross is the measure of love, and I wish to love you crucified, and beyond all measure.

Will you hear me, O my Jesus here present with me? O, yes, you ever answer the fervent prayers of the loving heart, which longs to suffer and immolate itself for you unreservedly. Give me that love, I beg of you, which blooms only in the midst of crosses.

Amen.

7. «LORD, MAKE ME SEE»

Yes, Jesus of my soul, make me see! I am blind, Lord, and I ask for light to see your perfections and my weaknesses, to know you and to know myself, to fix my gaze on you and never to turn it away from that Host in which my life dwells.

I am blind, my Jesus, to the operations of your Divine grace, blind also to the multitude of my weaknesses.

I am blind and cannot see my self-love to its full extent, in all its ugliness. I am blind when it comes to recognizing my pride, my tendency to get upset over trifles, my stubbornness and my distaste for mortification.

Lord, if you want, you can cure me but how can I cure myself?

— By being humble, because blindness of heart proceeds from pride. Be humble and your eyes shall perceive your innumerable vices; be pure and you shall see God.

How can you know me, with your eyes covered with a thick veil of self-love? How can you gaze on me with your heart sullied by touchiness and pride, and by attachment to your own opinion?

Blessed are the pure in heart, for they shall see God, I said one day, and if you want to know me, study me and contemplate me . . . if you want to know yourself, be humble and pure, pure in body and pure in soul.

Learn to know yourself and to despise yourself. Think often about your nothingness. Consider your weaknesses, your lack of strength, your negligences and your innumerable infidelities. Never think yourself better than your neighbor. Always believe that your brother is better than yourself, and excuse his faults and look upon his virtues with the eyes of charity.

Despise no one, my child, and cast far from you every desire to be loved and admired.

Never pause to wish to be sought after, to be consulted, to gain approval . . . never prefer your opinion to that of others.

When you are reproved do not excuse yourself. Never speak of yourself, nor say anything to show yourself in a favorable light. On the contrary, speak joyfully of what will demean you in the eyes of others, and rejoice at being always the last, at serving and not at being served . . .

Thus, My beloved son, you shall cure the blindness of your soul; thus shall you see the light, and what is more, Him who is the Light of light. It is through the glasses of humility that you shall be able to look at me.

— Thank you, my adorable Jesus! From this very moment I will put into practice your heavenly counsels. I will humble myself in order to see you, and on seeing you I shall be so much entranced with your beauty, as never to leave you again. That is what I ask and wish to obtain, through Mary's intercession. Amen.

8. «MAN DOES NOT LIVE
BY BREAD ALONE»

I wish my food to be the doing of your will, O my Jesus, that adorable will which is to constitute my whole life. I wish, O Lord, your will to be a Paradise for me, in spite of the sacrifices I am called upon to make. But what matters if I endure them for love of You?

When I think of you, all my troubles vanish, all my fears are at and end, and all immolation seems to be sweet when I see in it an expression of your will.

Lord, give me of that spirit and deliver me from all sensuality.

I wish to renounce everything in which my body would find pleasure; never seeking enjoyment either within or without; not looking for any satisfaction or for the applause of men. Without all this my protestations of love would be nothing but illusion.

Lord! If I did not love mortifications, I would have reason, in a certain sense, to despair. I must be ingenious, O my Jesus, in punishing myself, in renewing my sacrifices unceasingly, in order to attain that spiritual life, that Divine life which is the nourishment of the soul.

O Jesus! here present with me in the Sacred Host! I need that life of intimacy with you, that constant presence of the Beloved One. I want to live and breathe in your most Sacred Heart.

I have need of you, O my Jesus, to live, to be pure, to sanctify myself. I wish for no other bread, but the bread of life which takes away all hunger and all thirst: that immortal bread, which opens the gates of heaven to those who partake of it.

I have no wish to live on the food which the world offers to me. I long ardently for the food of the saints, the food which produces virgins, which feeds us in a Divine manner, and this food which is the bread of the soul, is yourself, my beloved Savior, whom I ardently desire to receive each moment, at every respiration, and at every pulsation of my heart.

I do not live on material things which dissipate and dry up the spirit. I was not born to feed on earthly things, and all that is not you, O my beloved Jesus, is of the earth, earthly!

But is it possible that God should make his dwelling in a body so vile, in a soul so earthly, so wretched and so ungrateful? Ah, yes, happily for me, all this is divinely true! Man separated himself from God, and the God of heaven came to make himself man, to unite God with man, and man with God.

My God, My God, how and with what heart shall I be able to show my gratitude for so much goodness? . . .

Amen.

9. WHAT WILL YOU, LORD?

Speak, my Jesus, your poor servant hears you. I, whose sole happiness consists in pleasing you, desire only to know your will, that I may hasten to accomplish it.

Do you wish me to suffer spiritually and physically, and that my heart should be submerged in an ocean of sorrows? I wish to suffer that I may be transformed into you.

Is it your wish to give me consolations, and joys, and that I should be loved and esteemed for qualities it seems to me I do not possess? Then it is my wish likewise, my loved Jesus! since I have no other desire except to do your Divine Will at every moment.

I love the cross, my Jesus, not so much because it is the cross, as because I see in it your will which I adore!

O most holy Will, Love of all my loves! How I love You! Make me understand it, in order that I may accomplish it in every detail.

Do you wish me to live passively, while I am evolving in my innermost heart innumerable plans for your glory? I accept this passivity, this impotence, while remaining a martyr of my desires, for love of you.

I wish to bind myself to you by a complete offering of my entire being, soul, body, life, senses and powers. I give up all claim to myself; that is to say, the conception that any of these things belong to me.

My Jesus! I do not wish to possess any longer anything of my own, and I shall only make use of any right I have to these things, in order to sacrifice them to you; for I wish to renounce myself and immolate my will to yours forever.

But tell me, Lord, what you want of me, what you desire of me; for I am ready to listen to your divine voice, and to obey you without delay.

— My son, I wish your heart to be empty of creatures, empty of yourself.

I wish to be the only object of your desires and of your love.

I demand from you the utmost fidelity in my Service. It is your wish to resign your will to mine; to do all you can to please me. Do you know what is the ardent longing desire of your Jesus? I have but one desire, one only, my beloved son. It is to find those souls who, in union with me, will offer themselves in sacrifice, as victims for the sins of the world.

That is what I ask of you, my son: forgetfulness of yourself and zeal for the salvation of souls: an angelic purity, and a never ceasing martyrdom for those souls that are steeped in sin.

I wish you to be as a chain in order to form a barrier to keep back those who approach the abyss. I wish this community to be a sort of oasis where my heart shall find consolation and where many will find repose.

I ask for love, purity, suffering: I ask for your soul, that soul I love so much.

Amen.

10. LOVE

O, Jesus, Divine Word of my life, of my existence, of all my being, you who absorbs me, who fills me with admiration, and with ecstatic love, who unites me to yourself, who overwhelms me with your incomprehensible abasement, O my Jesus, what shall I say to you?

Oh Lord, let me tell you that I perceive and feel your presence, that I possess you, that I touch you, that I adore you, that I love you! O yes, a thousand times I will repeat that I love you, and that I am dying because I cannot love you more, much more, infinitely more!

I have no other love but you, my supreme Good, my Life, my heaven, my only desire; and all other loves, great but with human limitations, although pure and legitimate in their origin, because sanctified by contact with you, all these loves are also yours, my Jesus!

I feel lost and, as it were, absorbed in your Heart, O Jesus! Master of my whole life! My whole being is consumed with an ardent love for you. I am on fire, I burn, and know not, O my God, why I am not reduced to ashes at your approach.

I look and look, and turn to look again at that consecrated Host; its whiteness dazzles me; its brilliant rays wound my soul to its utmost depths by revealing to me all its defects and deformities.

Who can call himself pure in the presence of Purity itself? Who is without spot before the spotlessness of Jesus?

Who can think himself humble in the presence of him who is hidden under the form of bread?

Who can say that he suffers in the presence of the Man of Sorrows?

Who will believe himself innocent before the immaculate Lamb?

Who, finally, will dare to call himself a martyr before the sacred victim of Calvary?

O, my Lord! in your presence, I ought to feel nothing but shame and a deep sense of my utter worthlessness; but I also feel great love for you; a burning love, which in uniting me to you, consumes all the vileness of my poor heart; a love which purifies and transforms me, and takes me far away from this earth to that purest of Hosts, the very abode of Love.

Amen.

11. I THINK OF YOU

How could it be otherwise, for you are my Love, O my Jesus in the Holy Eucharist? My first thought on waking is of you, beloved of my soul, and my last before closing my eyes in sleep, is of that consecrated Host, with an ardent longing for the dawn of another day when I can approach you and receive you again in Holy Communion.

And it is not only on these two occasions that I think of you, my adorable Jesus, but at every beating of my heart I look for you; at every breath, and at every pulsation of my heart, I ardently long for you, and offer to you my love and my life!

I think of you before dawn . . . even before the birds have begun to salute you with their morning song. I think of you in the midday heat; and when the shades of night surround me, the remembrance of you and of your love is what affords me the brightest of lights.

O Jesus of the Eucharist! O consecrated Host! O envied Monstrance! O blessed Ciborium, beloved of my heart! The Tabernacle is my Treasure and, far or near, my eyes never lose sight of it, for it contains the God of Love.

I dream of you, my Jesus, in the sacrament of your Love, and you are the joy of my heart from the first moment of my waking. If I pray it is to seek you. If I make sacrifices it is to please you.

In my sorrows I think of you, and my joys are bitter if you do not share them.

When I see you outraged or offended, my heart is torn asunder, and when I see you praised, my joy is beyond measure.

How can I forget him, who is the sole object of my thoughts, the King of my mind and of my heart?

How can I for a single instant forget my Jesus, so gentle, so divine, so loving, so pure? O, the infinite charm, and the entrancing beauty of Jesus!

If I thought, O my good Jesus, that all the tortures of martyrdom increased a thousand fold, could draw even a smile from you or could give you the smallest pleasure, I would face them all without a moment's hesitation and with all my heart.

This mode of loving you is, as it were, the very essence of my life. It is my mission to console you, O my Jesus, to forget myself in thinking only of You. The great secret is not to think of myself, in order always to think of you. In this way, and only in this way, can I think of you by forgetting myself. You shall take my place, I repeat, in my thoughts, and in my very heart.

Grant me ever this grace, Lord of my life, to think of you so often that I cannot even live or breathe if I forget you for a single moment.

Amen.

12. «GO AND SIN NO MORE»

«Go and sin no more». This is what Jesus says to me every time I go to confession.

How great is the goodness of heart of my Beloved, and I wish to respond to his delicacy towards me with a pure soul, the life of a martyr, and the heart of an angel!

These words of our Lord touch me to the quick. How delicate is the heart of Jesus, such love and such tenderness could proceed only from God!

And how do I respond to his wonderful goodness? What are the fruits derived from my confessions?

Do I not always come back with the same sins, the same defects, the same imperfections?

Can I truly say that since I heard those sweet words of Jesus, I have not fallen again into sin?

Have I preserved that peace of soul which a tranquil conscience alone can give, or have I allowed it to be taken from me in a thousand different ways?

Have I not often misused that Sacrament by which the soul is reinvigorated, purified, and refreshed in the very blood of the spotless Lamb?

How often when kneeling at the feet of the priest, have I not sought rather to obtain consolation than to repent and weep over my sins! Alas, how often also, in that holy place have I not sought my own gratification! How often have I feared to lay bare all my weaknesses!

How often have I excused my imperfections, spoken ill of others, and sought to please my confessor without giving a thought to that contrition and voluntary humiliation, which should always accompany my confession!

And, perhaps, on several occasions, I have made use of the very faults I was accusing myself of, for that end. I have sought to be praised, preferred, and to be excused, and when I did not find this, I got up and went sadly away, with sorrow in my heart, because my self-love was left unsatisfied.

O my Jesus! O Sacred Host! How can I avoid blushing with shame at the foot of this altar before your gaze so infinitely pure?

Pardon me, Lord. Pardon me for my lack of delicacy towards you and for my exceedingly great pride, which manifests itself even in the most sacred things.

Covered with shame and confusion, I undertake, O my Jesus! to sin no more. At your feet in the Sacrament of Penance, I, a penitent sinner, will humbly implore your infinite mercy.

I will be direct and open, and will ask you unceasingly for that grace, which is so uncommon «to walk straight before the Lord and to be sincere with Him».

Who would believe it? And yet it is but the bare truth that I have not been loyal to him. But I will be so in the future and I must obtain this grace at all costs, through the intercession of Mary, my Mother.

Amen.

13. «TO WHOM SHOULD WE GO?»

«You have the words of eternal Life», and I will listen to no other voice but yours, Jesus the God of my soul! Away from me all worldly sounds, far from me all the echoes which come from earth!

Only you, O my Jesus, Life of my life, speak to my heart. O divine Speech, O beloved Word! May human beings cease speaking to me, may their flattering and lying tongues no longer find an echo in my soul!

May I no more listen to the evil one and to his malignant temptations of pride, spite and envy!

May I no more listen to myself, my beloved Lord, with my exaggerated self-love, my foolish imagination and my uncontrollable passions, which plunge me into trouble, darkness and dismay!

O beloved Host! O my Jesus meek and humble of heart! Speak to my heart and calm the storms which agitate it.

Say but a word, and peace will return to it.

Speak, my Lord, speak; your poor servant listens to you, one word from you and my soul shall be saved.

To whom shall I go, Life of my life, if not to you who are the Life Eternal?

Who but you can understand me, my beloved Lord? Who can give me light, grace, warmth, hope, and all other virtues, who but you who are all charity and tenderness and love itself?

When I feel immersed in an ocean of sorrow, when the waters of tribulation inundate my soul, where shall I seek for a haven of rest, but in your heart, O my beloved Lord?

When my soul is sad and weary through desolation and abandonment, where shall I find refreshment, and peace, if not in your most precious blood, which rejoices the soul by the visits of its grace.

When I am overcome with weakness and discouragement, when temptations surround me on every side, to whom shall I have recourse, but to him who is consolation and strength itself?

When pride threatens to invade my soul, when attachments torture me, and self-love increases within me all these trials and difficulties . . . to whom shall I turn, O my beloved Jesus, but to you, who are the Lamb of God, so humble, so gentle and kind, so full of tenderness, sweetness and love?

And when my soul is flooded and filled with consolation, and peace and happiness reign in my heart, to whom shall I go, if not to you, O my Jesus, that I may share my joy and happiness with you.

On every occasion, O my beloved, it is to you that I wish to go; it is upon your most loving Heart that I wish to lean, both now and through eternity.

14. «WITHOUT ME, YOU CAN DO NOTHING» . . . «I CAN DO ALL THINGS IN HIM WHO STRENGTHENS ME»

How true this is! I am nothing but impotence and weakness; but with grace and faith and love, I am capable of doing all, when with these helps, I realize my nothingness and distrust my weakness, and remember that I am «dust».

But how shall I obtain that faith which removes mountains, that grace which is so powerful and that love which soars above all creatures and things?

It is by prayer, for it is in prayer alone that is found hidden those holy graces which are the commencement of our eternal life.

When God works in a soul in order to sanctify it, he makes it become simple. And it is solely by prayer, by the giving up of its own will, by stripping itself of all excess in the use of creatures, and by restraining and mortifying itself in all its faculties, that this can be accomplished.

Those who walk with giant strides on the road to perfection are they who advance with simplicity before God; who strive to please him by keeping themselves always meek and humble.

«Teach me, Lord, what you wish me to say to you», the Blessed Margaret Mary exclaimed one day.

«Nothing else», answered Jesus, but this: «My God, my One and my All».

One life would not be sufficient; indeed, we would require a thousand lives, in order to have time to penetrate and understand fully the meaning of these beautiful and divine words.

If, said Saint Jane of Chantal, we could fathom the real meaning of these words, «My God and my All», we would never feel weary during our prayers and meditations, for at the first signs of weariness these words would transport us again with joy!

«God is all, and I am nothing!» Repeating these words, St. Francis of Assisi passed whole days and nights in the highest contemplation!

And why, O my God, cannot I remain at your feet, during my hours of love and adoration, and repeat again and again without ceasing and without tiring:«I myself am nothing, and can do nothing, but with the grace of God I can do all».

Lord, give me this spirit of prayer that I may obtain every virtue, through the grace which it will pour into my soul.

«If God grants you nothing in your prayers», said St. Francis of Sales, «if you can do nothing else, adore him, adore his presence . . . his mysterious ways . . . his wise and loving operations in your soul: to do this it is not necessary to have great thoughts, nay, indeed it is better to adore him in silence, than to reason much».

If you can do absolutely nothing, suffer in silence, for what you cannot do by working, you will do by suffering. Therefore, when we can do nothing, let us embrace and kiss the Cross, and press it to our hearts; for if we can do nothing of ourselves, one day when the hour of grace shall have come, when God in his wisdom and love sees best, then, in truth, shall we be capable of doing great things for him.

Amen.

15. «I AM THE LIGHT OF THE WORLD»

Yes, my Jesus, «he who follows you does not walk in darkness». You are the Light of my soul, of my heart, and of my eyes. You are the Light of my life, and God of my soul. The Divine Light which radiates from you bathes my soul and penetrates it through and through whenever I receive you in your Sacrament of Love.

You are, O my God, the Eternal Light whose celestial rays illuminate and brighten the paths of my life.

You are to me as a rainbow of hope amid the thick black clouds which darken the horizon.

Throughout the «dark night of my soul» you are my Hope, O my adorable Jesus! And when my soul passes through cold and lonely regions it is with you that I find light and warmth.

The world is lost because it has fled from your light and fears to approach lest its deformity be visible; for «it hates the Light that its works may remain hidden».

The souls that are filled with the spirit of the world, walk in darkness, because they shun the Cross; for the Cross is Light, it is a burning fire, and it breathes forth love, for Jesus Himself has made himself one with it. Therefore, he who avoids and flees from the cross, flees also from Jesus, and, when Jesus is absent, there is nothing but blindness and sin!

And, alas, how much blindness there is in the world, and even in religious houses, when they do not love the Cross and have a dread of sacrifice!

These souls are not inflamed with love by the holy wood of the cross, that divine and lively fuel. They are entirely engrossed in the lying and foolish pleasures of the world, which make their darkness still darker and more obscure.

O Cross, O blessed Cross, O Cross well beloved! Truly, my heart is on fire with a most ardent desire to clasp you in my arms. I wish only to become one with you, and I desire no other treasure on earth than cross after cross, and sorrow upon sorrow. Grant, O my Jesus, that these crosses without number may rest within my soul!

I wish to suffer in order that the light from heaven above may enlighten me and cause me to shine in the next life in glory. «I hunger and thirst» after sufferings, in order that I may fill up the measure of sorrow which has fallen to my lot.

There is a void in my soul, O my Eucharistic Jesus, which nothing here can fill, an insatiable thirst for suffering and martyrdom, an ever-increasing desire and longing for sacrifice, an ardent yearning for the Cross, which is my Light.

«I have come to cast fire on the earth, and what will I, but that it be kindled?» But this fire is enkindled by the wood of the Cross. How, then, will I be able to desire anything, but to be fastened and nailed to it?

O Light of the World, Light of my soul, my Jesus crucified! Nail me on the other side of your own Cross, and there with the diverging rays of your heart of Fire, enlighten my intelligence that I may know you and know myself . . . in order that I may love you and hate myself.

Amen.

16. «I WILL NOT LEAVE YOU ORPHANS»

— O my child, son of the Cross and of my Heart: your father and mother may fail you, but I will never abandon you!

Even at my death I did not leave my children orphans, for day and night they can find me on their altars.

With the tenderness and gentleness of a thousand mothers, the Last Supper came to sweeten the bitterness of Calvary; for I knew that in the Holy Eucharist you would always have with you a father and a mother, and would never be alone while on earth . . .

And, therefore, although my Passion caused me excessive sufferings, yet I found consolation and relief in the thought that I was to leave myself to you in the Holy Eucharist.

I wished, my beloved child, that my body, which was crushed under the burden of the cross, and my blood, which was shed for all mankind, should be, within the Sacrament, your consolation and joy.

I wished it . . . my dearly beloved child. In those supreme moments of indescribable anguish, the thought that you would be happy in the possession of the Holy Eucharist increased my strength during My passion, and lessened My fear. And that is why the Institution of this Holy Sacrament immediately preceded My greatest sufferings.

It could not be otherwise, my dearly beloved child, than that the thought of always living by your side would lessen and alleviate My sufferings.

It was this thought that caused me to sing the song of thanksgiving with joy as I walked with my Apostles to the Garden of Olives. And during the painful moments of my Passion, I had continually before my mind those sweet hopes which had been with me during the Last Supper.

When my body was being scourged cruelly . . . and when my blood was pouring on the ground, I rejoiced, my dearly beloved son. I rejoiced at being ground like wheat in the mill and pressed like grapes in the winepress, thus making myself the bread and the wine to nourish you at the Eucharistic banquet.

Before death had taken me away from men, I had disposed and arranged to multiply my life upon their altars.

Do you not see then my child, that even in dying I have not left you as an orphan; for every day and at every moment of the day, from one end of the world to the other, these words of my Priests rise to Heaven: «*This is My Body. This is My Blood*»; and I rejoice at being a constant victim for love of you.

— O Jesus, O my beloved Jesus! O Jesus hidden here beneath these Sacramental veils! Grant that at every moment of my life I may return gratitude and love to you for your great love for me!

O Mary, my Mother, our Lady of the Eucharist! Help me to offer thanks to Jesus, and always to prepare myself perfectly to receive him with a love like yours.

Amen.

17. «GIVE ME OF THIS WATER»

O Lord, I long to drink of waters which will quench my thirst forever. I thirst for the blood and the water which flowed from your side, which will nourish and purify my soul.

I thirst for humiliations and for sacrifices . . . I thirst for crosses and for Calvary. I thirst for Heaven and for the Eucharist. I thirst for love. I thirst for you who are the Life of my life. I thirst for you who are as an Ocean of hope to me, a river to bring me infinite graces, the profound source of the science of the Cross, and the spring of every consolation and the fountain of all that is pure.

O Jesus, O my well-beloved Jesus. You are an ocean of beauty, grandeur, tenderness and sweetness; of light, consolation, and untold joy. You are the Rose born of Mary, God's mystical Rose. The Lily born of Mary, God's pure white lily, O Jesus, Son of Mary.

Won't you, my Jesus, quench my thirst, so that I may never thirst again, you who are an Ocean, and the source of Love, and the stream from where that love flows to me.

You are *my Jesus!*
Greatest of the Great!
Gentlest of the Gentle!
Purest of the Pure!
Tenderest of the Tender!
Beauty of all Beauty!
Light of all Lights!
Comforter of all Comforters!
Delight of all Delights!
Love of all Love!

You are all this and indeed much more, O my dear Divine Lord! How could I not thirst for you, my Heaven of Heavens? I thirst for you in your Tabernacle. I thirst for you on the Cross. The Communion and the Cross will calm and satisfy this insatiable thirst which lives and burns within me.

I wish I could receive you at every beating of my heart, my Jesus, at every breath I draw! I wish I could crucify myself and renounce my own will at every moment of my life! I long to remain constantly at the foot of your Cross, that I may be washed and cleansed in that divine and Precious Blood which flows from your Heart . . . I pine for love . . . I pine for sufferings! . . .

O my Jesus present within the Host, in your tenderness and pity, calm and quiet within me these ardent yearnings for suffering and for love.

I thirst, o my God, for those virtues which I do not possess . . . I have a thirst, my Jesus, a burning thirst to win back souls to love you and adore you; to obtain for you souls who will find all their joy in crucifying themselves and suffering for Love of You. This thirst, O my Jesus, is killing me.

Calm it, for pity's sake, by giving me thousands of souls which I may offer and give to you.

I thirst above all to quench your thirst, O Jesus, by presenting you with thousands of perfect souls. I thirst to comfort and console you, since you seek this comfort from me in the Host, your abode of Love.

The world fills you with sorrow, O my Jesus, and I would give you of that water which is distilled from the Cross, and which is made up of purity and love. This shall be your comfort and refreshment, o my Jesus. But first give it, you yourself to me, that I may have the joy of offering it to you, and at the same time quench the thirst which consumes me!

Amen.

18. «JUDGE NOT THAT YOU BE NOT JUDGED»

These are the words of our divine Lord while he was here upon earth. Have I been faithful in carrying out this precept? Have I always been charitable towards my neighbor?

And even towards God himself? Have I sometimes been so presumptuous as to sit in judgment on his dealings with me, and questioned his love and justice in the daily events of my life? And when I have hidden these sentiments from others, have I not been guilty of cherishing them within myself?

Have I always interpreted charitably with kindness the actions of others?

Have the acts of my superiors[2] never been the subject of my criticisms?

Have I subordinated my private judgment to others and given up my own ideas and will with perfect obedience and docility?

---

[2] The context here is Fr. Felix's religious community where it is important that the authority of the superior not be undermined by critical remarks behind his back.

Have I in the presence of others offered an opinion contrary to theirs, believing it to be better, more opportune, and more prudent?

O my God! Indeed, I cannot do anything but blush with shame when I see my guilt in so many forms.

"Judge not. God alone has the right to judge." A thousand times I have read this, and yet can I say that I have been more vigilant in controlling my imagination and in mastering my tongue?

"With the same measure that you shall measure, it shall be measured to you," also said our divine Lord, and I tremble, O my Jesus, at the thought, for I am indeed so guilty.

O my dearly beloved Jesus! Let the abundant merits of your Cross remove my guilt. Forget my ingratitude. Cast my crimes into the depths of the sea. Conceal forever my want of loyalty. Blot out my sins for pity's sake with your most precious blood, and forgive me all those many rash judgments and unkind interpretations which I have so often committed.

How many of these rash judgments and how many of these mistakes have I cause to regret! Therefore from this day forward, I will only judge myself and that without pity. I will only see the beam in my own eye, that I may not see the splinter in my brother's.

Give me that charity, Lord, which is something Divine, rather than something human; that goodness and kindness which is the noblest part of ourselves, which shuts its eyes to the faults of others; which lessens and forgets the wrong they may do.

I must make war on my defects and not become accustomed to them. And I must fight against and overcome this tendency which I find within myself to judge others and think of others in unkind ways.

I will see the image of God in everyone whom I meet. And I will love them as Jesus loves each one of us. In this is to be found the great secret of charity.

O Mary, my Mother, who never judged anyone, who imitated Jesus in being a model of the most perfect charity, obtain for me the grace always to see in my neighbors the good qualities which they have received from God, and a holy charity that may always hide their imperfections from me.

Amen.

19. LOOK

How can the soul look upon Jesus, hidden in his Sacrament of Love, without being over-whelmed with shame?

Only when the soul loves him; when it has always been pure, or has just been purified, and when it has sacrificed and humiliated itself for love of him.

The soul which is filled with pride, sensuality and sin, can never look upon Jesus, nor fix its gaze on him without a sense of shame.

The soul must have acquired the highest virtue in order to be able to unite itself to Jesus by means of these looks of love.

Humility: for no one is worthy to look at Jesus.

Purity: for the Lord turns his eyes away from all that is unclean.

Poverty of Spirit: for God does not look at, nor does he allow himself to be seen by, nor does he ever descend into, the soul which does not believe it has need of him.

Obedience: for this virtue alone gives us the docility of children, and Jesus said «Allow the little children to come to me».

Suffering: for Jesus looks for that mark, that special quality which gives the souls who come and adore here at his feet a likeness and image of himself. He looks for the mark of sacrifice in souls . . . in their bodies, in their senses . . . in their faculties, as also in their hearts. And when he finds it, he is filled with joy.

Our Eucharistic God cannot remain unmoved when he sees the mark of the Cross on those who come to visit him. He smiles as he looks upon them and cannot turn away his eyes from this chosen band who voluntarily resemble him nailed on a Cross.

And I, who have professed to love the Cross, and whose vocation it is to adore Jesus night and day; when I kneel at the foot of the altar with these lighted candles being consumed before me, can I truly say that I bring joy to the heart of Jesus?

Am I humble, pure, mortified, poor, obedient, and really attached to the Cross in whatever form it comes? Crucifying myself in order to become more and more like Jesus, out of love for him?

Have I the disposition of a little child in order that I may be worthy to come and contemplate Jesus . . . to listen to the divine and tender words which fall from his lips . . . to approach and draw near to him with affection and love . . . to hide myself in the folds of his Sacred robe . . . to draw light, grace, life, fire, love from his loving heart, and all virtues for myself and for others?

Meditate on this, O my soul, and repent of your faults reflect on what you ought to do, the means you must choose that correspond with the love and goodness of your Jesus. And as you withdraw from the altar, cast a look of love and gratitude upon the Sacred Host where Jesus dwells in love for you.

O Mary, my dear Mother, obtain for me the grace that I may ever keep my eyes upon Jesus, as you loved to do when you were here on earth!

Amen.

20. CHARITY

Behold hidden within the Sacred Host, O my beloved Jesus, the virtue which I need above all others! My soul thirsts for charity: for that clear crystal water of charity which rests within your Sacred Heart as within a deep unfathomable well. I come to drink at this pure and holy Source that I may be cleansed, and may be blessed, and may receive life from it, and light and love.

You, O my God, are the source of all charity. O how I long to possess this virtue that I may know how to have compassion on the weaknesses and frailties of my neighbors . . . that I may overlook their defects . . . pardon their faults, and forget their ingratitude.

O my beloved Jesus! How shall I act in the midst of so many faults and imperfections which I meet without cease in the lives of those around me? Have I to endure their wounding and unkind manner of making requests and the manifold evil consequences of uncontrolled human passion to which our poor human nature is prone?

— Always with charity, my son, ever having before your eyes your divine model who spent his life while here on earth in going about doing good. Of him it was said: «Goodness has appeared in our land», and who himself said «Learn of me for I am meek and humble of heart».

— Do you ask me how you must consider the faults of your neighbor, my child?—Always with purity of intention, that is to say, without passion . . . without bias . . . seeing the creature in God and God in his creature.

Often dwell upon the good qualities which you see in others . . . It is necessary for you always to keep a watch over yourself, to be master of yourself, to turn away your eyes and, in unruffled calm, to let pass the little annoyances which may come to you from those around you, recommending them all the time to God.

With the profoundest humility you should think that you are or might be much worse were it not for all the graces received from me.

When a particular person commits some fault, you should think that he was taken by surprise, was off his guard, so as to be easily tempted by the evil one. You could think of the possibility that he did not have sufficient light and that I permitted it in order to exercise and perfect your virtues. And why not?

Lift yourself, my son, high above all these human weaknesses of which you also are full. Keep your conversation always in heaven and dwell with me above. Think not of these things which trouble and vex you below.

Learn to be humble, kind, and gentle, for that is the way I wish you to be.

Strive never to come into my presence with your soul stained with sins against charity. Courage, my dear son. Practice each day these two virtues of charity and humility, and I will be with you to help you.

O Mary, my Mother, of all creatures the most charitable, pray for me and help me to love my neighbor as myself for the love of God!

Amen.

21. «MANY ARE CALLED»

But why are there so few chosen, my Jesus?

Why, out of a thousand souls called by you to a life of perfection, are there so few who respond to your call?

— Because they do not love the Cross or a life of sacrifice . . . the idea of suffering appalls them . . . because they do not love me enough.

I call them, my dear son, I call them to the highest perfection, but how few there are who listen and who keep their hearts pure and their ears attentive to my voice? Very few are they, alas, who are detached, humble and mortified, who give themselves to me unreservedly, and who respond to my call by allowing themselves to be molded as I will.

The souls who are the chosen ones are those who are humble of heart: I love these souls with a special love. To them I give light to know themselves, to convince themselves of their own nothingness, and to be happy in that thought. They understand that they deserve hell a thousand times, and that if they escape from it, it is only owing to God's grace and to the help given them by those charitable souls who have assisted them. Their pride does not resist these thoughts so full of justice.

They see clearly their spiritual poverty, their weaknesses, their nothingness. They place within my hands all that in justice belongs to me, and remain joyful and happy in the thought of their poverty and nothingness.

My dearly beloved son, such are the souls who are chosen and who are specially beloved by me. They are those who have understood the language of the Cross, and have put it into practice; who are dead to themselves and to their own self-will, and who live my life of victim, abandoning themselves entirely to my will.

Do you wish to follow me quite closely?

Take up the Cross and renounce yourself for love of me. The chosen souls are also those who love a hidden life; who pass through the world unseen and unknown, and who fill the heavens with the perfume of their virtues.

My chosen ones are also pure, detached from all things earthly and material as a result of repeated victories over themselves. They are detached from everything here on earth and always forgetful of themselves. Pure of heart, they cannot but love since they bear within themselves the source of love, God himself.

O my beloved son, heaven gazes with love on the soul entirely pure, and the Holy Spirit reposes in it as on a bed of roses.

Do you wish, my son, to be among those called to perfection, and to be specially loved by me? Then be pure, be loving, be a martyr. Then you shall have «your heart's desire».

Love with tenderness your Mother Mary, and pray to her each moment for guidance and protection. Love even unto frenzy, and suffer even unto martyrdom.

Amen.

22. SOULS! SOULS!

This is the cry of my heart whenever I approach your Tabernacle, O my Jesus! It is also the echo of your divine and loving Heart which is constantly resounding in mine. O my Eucharistic Jesus! My greatest suffering is at the thought that you asked me for these souls and that I haven't a million at my disposal to offer you.

All the things that I see, that I hear and that I touch all seem to repeat the cry for souls, souls! That cry awakens me at night. O Lord of my life, I have none to offer you but one which is my own, but which is ready to offer itself in sacrifice in order that millions of others may be saved and obtain your glory.

How hard it is for the heart that loves you and is full of zeal for the salvation of souls to be unable to exercise it. What a cruel martyrdom!

O grief, above all other pains, to see my Jesus outraged, forsaken, wounded and despised by those souls ransomed by him!

Can I, alas, present myself before this altar with a conscience free from reproach?

Haven't I on many occasions wounded your loving Heart with my many faults and my ingratitude?

Where are the proofs of my love for you? What have I done in the past for you? Where are the victories over my evil inclinations?

You, my Jesus, have proven your love for me by your humiliations, your labors, your thorns, your nails, your silence and your love! And I, what have I done? I am ashamed to tell you. You know what I have been and what I am now. But with your grace, in the future I will console you by my purity, my humility, and my self-denial. If I am unable to make other souls perfect, I will at least perfect my own in order that you yourself may become reflected in it.

But, even though I do not deserve it, give me pure and simple souls, full of fortitude and courage, and souls full of love for the Cross, so that I may be able to return them to you.

I am nothing but dust and ashes. But, O my beloved Lord, incline your ear and hear my prayer! Grant me today what I ask of you with so much ardor.

I beg you, O my Jesus, love those who do not love you. Open the doors of your Heart to those who do not knock. Heal those who inflame and aggravate their wounds instead of asking for the cure. O my Lord, look not on their blindness and ingratitude, but only upon the Precious Blood which you in love shed for them! Stop your enemies on the road of evil. Reveal to them your Divine love and mercy and save them. Since they will not go to you, go the them, my beloved Jesus, and in your tender pity forgive and pardon all.

In this way will you give me souls to give to you: in this way you will dry my tears in saving so many souls who are on the road to perdition. Yes, yes, my Jesus, may those souls be yours, even at the cost of my blood and my life; but, above all, have mercy on my soul which wishes to be yours forever!

Amen.

23. WHAT ENVY!

When I see the Angels who surround you, O my Jesus, I am filled with holy envy of their lot, because they are always by your side.

«I wish that I were an angel», is my frequent cry when the time comes, alas, to tear myself away from your side.

But an angel is purity itself. And am I an angel, being what I am? Verily, O Lord, I am not worthy to keep you company. And therefore, it is necessary for me to withdraw from you for a time.

But meanwhile, I can be an angel in other ways, at least. I will keep my soul white and pure that in this way I may be always ready to appear before you. I will guard you. I will stay with you. And I will remain with you in spirit night and day before this holy and consecrated Host.

My life shall be that of your Angels. I will always look upon you in spirit and discover in your eyes all your wishes and desires . . . I will do all the good that I can to the souls of those around me. I will weep as I think of all your sorrows, and rejoice with you when you do find millions of hearts to console your own most loving Heart.

I will imitate the angels, my Jesus, in bringing to your feet the sorrows of those who suffer, that you must comfort them . . . the faults of poor sinners, that you must pardon them . . . the virtues of those who love you, to give you joy, and also my own poor heart, that you may show compassion on it.

The angels have not my weaknesses. With their sublime intelligence they live by your breath, which gives life to all. They nourish themselves by feeding on your beauty, glory and light. But I eat your flesh and drink your blood each morning, in this way causing you to penetrate into the innermost recesses of my heart and my soul.

The angels see you face to face, but I receive your heart in mine. I feel it beating in my breast. Grant that its contact may give to my soul the whiteness and purity of the lily. O Jesus, hidden in the Sacred Host, how full of love you are who was willing to be happy not only in the company of angels but of men!

O my Lord! O wonderful thought! You have created heaven as a dwelling for the angels, and for your own dwelling, my poor heart! What shall I say to you? How shall I make a return for so much abasement and for so much love?

To become an angel, I know that I must live in close union with you in purity and light. Purify me, then, my Jesus, and change this darkness into light, so that I may not be too much ashamed in the presence of the angels who surround you.

I will be an angel. I will be thine, and with Mary, my Mother, purified and freed from all affections less pure.

Amen.

24. HUMILIATE ME

If I am to be transformed into your divine likeness, O my Jesus, it is necessary for me that you should send me humiliations frequently.

As long as my soul does not bear stamped on it the appearance of humility, I am very far from resembling you. And I wish to be an exact copy of you, although I do not deserve it.

I wish my natural and habitual state to consist in being crucified with you, in everyday seeking out new and fresh humiliations. O Jesus, my beloved Lord, give me real humility and a thirst for humiliations.

When will I lose sight of this self which meets me at every step of the way? «We shall never be anything before his Divine eyes, as long as we have any value in our own eyes». Therefore, from this day forward, will I not appraise myself at my true value, and humble myself, and treat myself as nothing, and disappear?

Strengthen in me, my Jesus, the low opinion I have of myself. Impress it on my soul. Make me more simpleminded for your mercy's sake, so that I may appreciate my utter nothingness and value as nothing all human praise and honor.

What am I but misery and wretchedness?

Can I do anything but evil and sin?

What am I worth? Nothing.

What do I possess but sins.

What do I deserve except Hell?

Being firmly convinced of all this, will I be capable of feeling elated about myself and of self-glorification?

What do I possess that I have not received?

How could a miserable sinner like me be puffed up with pride, O my Jesus?

O my God! If people knew me as I am, they would avoid me like a plague . . .

O yes, my Jesus, in your sight I desire to be something better than a whited sepulchre! . . . And so when my hour of adoration arrives, I cast myself at your Divine feet and, without ceasing, ask you to make me humble and to visit me with humiliations!

I know that to speak of Jesus is to speak of humility: for which reason my ardent desire is to possess this virtue. From now on, my greatest happiness will consist in seeing myself humiliated and despised. I will ardently endeavor to remain unknown and to feel that I am useless and without value.

I will never glory in anything but in my miseries, being fully convinced that I deserve neither affection nor esteem, and recognizing that I thoroughly deserve to be humiliated and despised.

I will never complain, Lord, nor find excuses for my faults. On the contrary, I will be happy and rejoice and will esteem it the most precious favor, if you will decide to allow me to be treated and trampled upon as the dust of the earth.

O my Jesus! O adorable Host! Preserve me from Hell, which I deserve for my sins.

O Mary, my good Mother, who always practiced humility in its most sublime form, and whose life passed in the greatest humiliation, obtain for me the grace to be like you and like Jesus, humiliated and despised.

Amen.

25. I AM SO POOR!

Yes, my Jesus! I am very poor in virtues; very poor in love for you. Therefore I come to you and say from the bottom of my heart: «*Behold, my Jesus, how poor I am!* Have compassion on my misery and comfort me in your mercy».

I am poor in humility, and in humiliations. Will you grant these to me? I am poor in patience and in victories over self. O my Jesus, grant to me today the grace to learn meekness and lowliness of heart from you.

I am poor in the virtues of silence, self-denial, charity and purity. I am poor, O my Jesus, in my love for the Cross, and for sufferings. And of these last mentioned virtues, perhaps my soul is in greater want than of any others.

Give me then, O my Lord, along with these virtues, the precious pearls of suffering . . . that fruit-bearing cross . . . those purifying sorrows, those interior trials which unite our two souls into one.

I would weep, Lord, in order to dry your tears . . . I would wish to be torn by thorns in order that I might heal and soothe your wounds. I wish to walk along the road to Calvary in order to follow and tread in your sacred footsteps. I wish for a cross that I may be crucified close by your side . . . I pine for the foolishness of the Cross, in order that it may make me more and more like you.

Lord, open your blessed hands and pour on me the treasure of voluntary suffering! I need blood, nails, wounds and humiliations. I am poor for lack of affronts, contempt, insults and calumnies, and I hunger for all these things. I hunger for them in order to resemble you, and that is why I wish to be crucified, and nailed upon a Cross like you. A soul that truly loves you, through love desires to suffer a lifelong martyrdom.

And I love you with such a love and desire to reproduce your sufferings in my own body and soul. I wish that at each moment of my life I may be immolated with you.

It is the Cross alone which forms the Saints, and I am, my own beloved Jesus, without a cross. I do not suffer and yet I am dying with an insatiable thirst for suffering.

O my Jesus, let me repeat it a thousand times: behold, my Jesus, how poor I am, and have compassion on me and send me your Cross and all your virtues!

O you, my King of Calvary, powerful and rich in sorrows, in humiliations and in tears! Through the love which you bear for your eternal and heavenly Father, grant some little donation to this poor soul, which desires to love you and to sacrifice itself for your honor.

O Mary, my good Mother, the richest of all creatures in sorrows, in contempt, in humiliations, in crosses of every sort, pray to Jesus for me. Get from him the same most precious favors for me!

Amen.

26. SUFFERING

O Jesus! O adorable Host!

I come to you today bathed in tears, with my heart shedding its blood drop by drop, and my soul plunged in an ocean of bitterness.

But what better preparation could I have to contemplate and understand you as a Victim in this most adorable sacrament? Were you not immersed yourself, O my Master, my only Love, in an ocean of sufferings . . . of weariness . . . and of fear . . . and of all that your Sacred humanity was capable of suffering, miraculously sustained by the Divinity itself?

And therefore, O my Jesus, the more bitter, the more profound, the more vast and the more agitated becomes this ocean of sorrows I am plunged in, the more I will rejoice. For in that way I shall resemble you the more, and I shall be the more pleasing to the Father, to the Holy Spirit and to you, the Word, who became incarnate for love of me.

It is certain, O my Jesus, that suffering is a grace . . . it is the very atmosphere of this dwelling, incensing your altar with its Divine perfume. Suffering purifies, and I wish to be pure. The tears which fall in your presence, during the hours of adoration, cleanse the soul and make it white, and I wish to be cleansed. O my Jesus, the thorns make the blood burst forth, and I wish to appear before your altar with my heart encircled with thorns, in order that I may take away the thorns that are in yours!

The Cross sanctifies, and I wish to become a Saint.

O Jesus Victim! I wish to become like you. I wish my soul to animate my body solely that I may be able to suffer in every way that is possible. I wish to love you and to forget myself. I wish to remember myself, but only that I may accept suffering at your hands for love of you.

What else can a victim desire but to immolate itself and to suffer more and more?

I love you in the midst of my sufferings. And should they increase and augment, I should know that I was loving you more! Accept my tears, O my Jesus, and my secret sorrows. I feel you are breaking the most delicate fibres of my heart one by one. But what is the difference, O my divine Physician? In your great love and mercy, finish the work you have begun in me.

It makes no difference that I weep, that my heart bleeds, and is torn asunder. Continue, O my good Lord, to cut into this metal until your features are engraved on it.

How beautiful, how sweet it is to suffer for him who has suffered so much for me!

O Mary, you have suffered for Jesus more than all other creatures put together; obtain for me the grace to imitate you at least a little, so that I may suffer for Jesus and for souls in carrying my cross after him until my last breath!

Amen.

27. AT DAYBREAK

The day is breaking, and with it comes the joy of joys: Jesus, who comes to fill my soul with roses and thorns, my path with flowers and tears, and my heart with graces and merits!

The light begins to dawn, and with it the Sun of my love will soon appear on the horizon.

The light of day, dissipating the darkness of night, finds me kneeling in silent adoration before him whom my soul loves best, Jesus, in the Sacrament of his Love.

The world wakes up, and I shudder at the thought that it wakes only to offend that hidden God whose only thought is to love and to sacrifice himself for sinners.

With the coming of the light I see the thorns piercing the Heart I adore . . . and I am sorely afflicted at seeing sacrilegious souls preparing the arrows with which to pierce your beloved Heart, O my Jesus!

O my God, at the thought of these crimes, I wish that I could keep back the light of day and continue to watch and console you, my Jesus, hidden in the night of your Tabernacle.

O that my love were capable of putting a stop to these sins! O that my prayers were powerful enough to prevent the blasphemies of man from reaching the ears of my Lord! But, alas, woe is me. What can I offer you, O my Jesus, in my poverty, except a heart that is consuming itself with love of you, but which is utterly incapable of consoling you?

Nevertheless, this poor heart will strive to become a victim of expiation. And, in uniting itself upon awakening to all saintly souls, it will rejoice in praising you and in singing with them hymns of praise and thanksgiving, while awaiting with an ardent desire the moment of receiving you.

I have watched over you in your sleep, O my Master! I have repressed the beating of my heart so as not to wake you, my beloved . . . but, behold, the day is breaking. Let me knock gently at the door of your Tabernacle and say to you with deep feeling: «Jesus, O my Jesus, awake, for I wish for no other dawn but your eyes; no other sun but your heart».

Come, Lord, I am eagerly longing to press you to my heart. The happy hour is fast approaching when you will be mine. I tremble with emotion at the thought of your approach and the moment when I shall look upon the brightness of your eyes. Come, my Jesus, for my heart is awaiting you with ardent desire, and is leaping for joy at the thought of possessing you!

The day has come and with it my Joy and my All!

Amen.

28. THIRTY MINUTES

How quickly do they pass, these thirty minutes of adoration before Jesus present in the Holy Eucharist! How quickly do the moments fly, my beloved, that I spend at the foot of your throne in the contemplation of your goodness, your love and your hidden virtues.

How short these minutes of heaven are for one who adores you, longs for you, sighs for your presence, loves you, consumes himself in loving you, thinks of nothing else but of pleasing you and is dying to remain at your feet to contemplate you! And yet how many precious acts of love can a soul elicit in a single moment when its love is ardent and intense!

In one moment one can make a perfect act of contrition . . . suppress an attachment which impedes one's spiritual advancement . . . humiliate oneself to any extent . . . weep over one's sins . . . One can save a soul, O my God, by sacrificing oneself in its favour, by offering the Eternal Word to the Father with all his infinite merits for that soul's conversion.

So many things I can do during my adoration! What graces I can obtain! What sins I can expiate!

And how supremely happy would those so many souls be if they, like me, had the incomparable privilege of passing hours at your feet. But what an account I will have to render you one day, O my God!

O my Jesus, make me understand how to appreciate and how to make use of these numerous graces which I am not worthy to receive. Grant me the grace to present myself before you in spotless purity. May my soul never be tarnished by a single intentional fault.

It is Angels who should surround your altar. How I would like to be as they are. I entered the religious life in order to be pure, my Jesus: To become a lily, a light, to be able without blushing to adore you, to love and contemplate you, to read your smallest wishes in your all pure eyes.

O incomparable love! O my beloved Jesus! Scarcely has my soul begun to open itself out to you when the thirty minutes are already gone. The painful hour of separation from you has already arrived. Hardly had I begun to entrust my sorrows to you, to offer you my promises, my intimate and loving disclosures, when the pitiless clock announces to me that I must depart and give up my place to a more fervent soul.

O my sweet Jesus. I wish I could stay the sun in its course, like Joshua, in order to have time to tell you how much I love you. But, an eternity would not be enough to express to you the intensity of my love.

Amen.

29. I SHALL NOT FORGET YOU

No never! All else my soul can forget. But you, my Jesus in the Eucharist, Life of my life, chosen among a thousand, my Good, my only One and my All; you I shall never forget!

How can I forget him to whom I owe my being and my life? How could I fail at every step, at every breath I draw, to remember him who is the very atmosphere around me, my dawn and my light?

Perhaps I will arrive, my Lord, at forgetting myself (what a joy if this should happen). But my crucified Master, never!

He is my father and my mother, my brother and my friend. He is my heaven on earth, more than my soul and my blood, my breath, and even my very heart! And this being so, can I ever forget him?

Can I make a single movement without him? Not when my memory recalls to me his exquisite qualities, my understanding points out his goodness, and my will, under love's direction, spring forth to accomplish his smallest wishes.

Whether open or closed, my eyes seek out Jesus, and in him alone find peace and repose.

My ears desire to listen only to his praises and to his Divine voice.

I wish «to taste him». I wish to possess him and press him to my heart, to satisfy myself with his sweetness, his purity, his beauty, and his Cross.

And, O adorable Host, where is the place where my soul has chosen to rest, if not on your throne, which is your Cross? What does it long for but for sufferings equal to yours? To what does it aspire but for your love?

Ah, no! Never shall I forget you, for you are the sweetness of my lips, the warmth of my life. It is you who make my heart beat. You are the director of my soul. In you are centered all my joys and all my desires. How then can I forget you, O my Jesus?

Is it not impossible to forget those one loves?

By your Eternal Truth you are the King of my intelligence. By your love, the King of my heart. And by your purity the King of my body.

What can I desire besides this consecrated Host? In all heaven and earth, what is there apart from you that can satisfy me? O sweetness, O beauty, O power of love!

What shall I do for you, O Jesus, Jesus of my soul! And what will you do for me?

We will never forget each other. I, in the contemplation of your love, and you, in your compassion for my weaknesses. I, in weeping for my sins, and you, in loving forgiveness for them. I, in never offending you any more, and you, in giving me your Heart forever!

O, how vehement is the love of my Jesus! Can I ever forget it? O no, never, never!

O most loving Mother of Jesus, who is also mine. Teach me and aid me in never forgetting our Jesus for a single instant!

Amen.

30.«HAVE COMPASSION ON ME»

For pity's sake, my Jesus, have compassion on me! I deserve to be no better than garbage in this community and an object of loathing to all. My soul is painfully distressed and I come to you in my rags to ask you for mercy.

All these years I have been in your service, my Jesus, and I am not yet either humble or mortified! My passions are as violent as on the day I became a novice. And how is it, O my Jesus, why is it that I make no progress but instead I feel I am losing ground?

— Alas! My beloved son, it all comes from the fact that you have not yet renounced yourself . . . On the way to perfection which love impels you to take, this renouncing is the first step.

If you do not renounce yourself, my son, it is because you do not love me, for the measure of your renouncing corresponds to the measure of your love.

My love demands several kinds of death. Renouncing yourself is love's field of battle.

If you did love me sincerely, you would forget yourself. If you really loved me, you would be burning with desire to resemble your Jesus crucified . . . If you really loved me, O my son, you would seek humiliations with all the passion of your heart, making them your food, and your life . . . If you really loved me, you would not count your sacrifices. You would rejoice in giving up your own will and in distrusting your own judgment.

Finally, if you really loved me, you would leave yourself . But what is it to leave yourself?

— It means to renounce yourself and to be dead to your own will . . . then you could even say No to your Yes and Yes to your No with a smiling face as you mortified your will.

All this depends on you, because although it hurts me to have to tell you this, the love that is needed depends on you!

Pride is your stumbling block, and as long as you have not conquered it by renouncing your own will and throwing yourself like a child into the arms of your superiors, you will remain in the same sad state you are at present.

Shake off this apathy which comes over you, my son. Burst apart the bonds of your own will which bind you to yourself. Then you will be freed from all ties so you can fly to Jesus. It is he who desires your perfection and hopes to see you die to yourself so that you have to live in him.

It is for this that you have come to this blessed spot; for this you possessed me in the Sacrament of my love. Come to me with all your infirmities and I will heal you.

Fear not. For a long time you have aroused my compassion and pity for you. Keep yourself humble I will allow myself to be pressed lovingly to your heart.

And, please Mary, also have compassion on me. Remember, my beloved mother, that it is for you to lead me to Jesus, for you are the Gate of Heaven!

Amen.

31. TO JESUS

What can I refuse you today? Nothing, because one can refuse nothing to the beloved. When one possesses Jesus in one's heart, is it possible to say, «No» to him?

Today my soul is ready, O my Jesus, to give you all you ask!

What do you want, my Jesus? What do you truly desire of me? Is it my interests—my health—my affections—my sufferings—my life, that you require?

— I desire your heart, my son, your heart full of the most perfect purity. For purity, you know, my son, is like the flower of love. And where love is, sin cannot exist.

This is my ideal: a garden of pure hearts, burning with a virginal love, white as lilies, growing around the Cross.

Purity, my son, is a flower of heaven. It grows only in the midst of thorns, and beneath the blessed shadow of the Cross.

There is no purity without voluntary sacrifice. Voluntary sacrifice exists only where there is love.

— But what is love? In what does it consist?

— In abandoning oneself and delivering oneself without reserve into the hands of God.

Love consists in depriving oneself of everything so as to have God as the sole occupant of one's heart.

For this I thirst in this corrupt world. I thirst for hearts that are completely empty and void of themselves so that I may fill them entirely with my presence. I thirst for purity and sacrifice, for generosity in my service. I thirst for self-renouncement. I thirst, in fact, for those Religious who are living crosses of love, purity and sacrifice!

And since you will deny me nothing today, my beloved son, renounce yourself, take up your cross and follow in my footsteps with a pure soul and a loving heart.

— O Jesus, you whose lily whiteness is bathed in blood! I will follow you. I will do what you will and what you ask, for today I can refuse you nothing.

O Mary, lily of purity, rose of love. Ask Jesus to give purity to your sons and your daughters .

Amen.

32. FOUR KINDS OF LOVE

How do I love you? I cannot tell you, my beloved Jesus. But I rejoice in asking you for love so that I can love you beyond measure with an incomparable love. This love will be far above all things and events, above all earthly affections, more than life or death, above myself, only wishing to forget myself and to be as if I did not exist. It will be a sublime, lofty, superior, pure, humble love which cannot be surpassed.

I wish, also, to love you, my Jesus, with an inseparable love. O, my beloved, this reminds me how closely you draw close to your creature, in order to receive the heart of man into your heart, his soul into your soul, his life into your own life.

I also wish to love you with a unique love, unique in its existence, unique in kind and form, unique in purity and sacrifice, unique in its quality, exceptional and indescribable! I want to love you with the love with which you have loved us; with that love, the heaven of all loves, the center of all things, the source of all lights, the sun of all rays.

I wish to love you also with an insatiable love; with a love that can never be satisfied, that always hungers and thirsts to love you more! O yes, insatiable in perfection, in degree, in trials and in martyrdom for the sake of the Beloved One, insatiable in its ardent desire to be voluntarily crucified.

I wish for a love so full, so ardent, so infinite that it can never be satisfied.

Give me, O my Beloved, these four kinds of love. Give them to me, O divine Jesus, I wish to burn and be consumed in this furnace of love.

Give me these four kinds of love, my Jesus, so I may have a more ardent desire of heaven. In this way my love for you will be more perfect, and above all, it will not decrease, but instead will continue to increase more and more until I die of pure love! Happily «love is stronger than death», and if I wish to suffer for my Beloved, love will offer me the most refined torments, the most hidden pains, and the most intense sufferings.

In this way I will love you, O my Jesus, and as long as I am on earth I wish to do nothing else but love you. He who loves, suffers; he suffers at being unable to love sufficiently him who is love.

I leave you, O my Jesus, but confidently expecting you to grant my requests.

O Mary, you who truly loved Jesus with an incomparable, inseparable, unique and insatiable love, make us love Jesus as you have loved him.

Amen.

33. «HOPE IN GOD!»

This is the cry of faith which is a constant source of strength for my soul! O, how full of consolation for me is the God of Hope!

Hope in God, is what a mysterious voice whispers to me when I am surrounded by tribulations . . . when bitter sorrows assail me . . . when my soul is tortured with anguish . . . when I feel abandoned and forsaken.

How sweet it is to hope against all hope, and to know that «he who hopes in God shall not be confounded forever».

You are my hope, O Jesus, in the Sacrament of your Love! If I am weak, you will give me strength! If I am hungry, you will feed me. If I am poor, you will provide for my needs. If I am sick, you will restore me to health.

O my Jesus, my most sweet Hope! If I am in darkness, it is you who will enlighten me. And here, in this holy home, I look to you for everything.

Clearly, he who hopes does so because he has not obtained all he hoped for. And I hope in God because I do not possess all I would like to obtain from him. I am poor in God, and I would be rich in the possession of him and his love. For he who has not love has not life, and I am without life!

O my good Jesus, my Hope and my consolation, my only Sovereign, Lord and Master! Being of my being, reposeful joy of my soul, search me today with one of those penetrating looks which sanctifies a soul in one instant! Incite me to virtue and sacrifice. I know there is no love where there is laziness, and that love is imperfect when it diminishes for lack of sacrifice.

«O ardent, O excellent and profound Charity of Christ», exclaimed St. Paul when he felt the cross bear more heavily on his shoulders. I envy your apostle, Lord, and I come to ask, and hope to obtain from you, a similar blessing.

To love and to suffer! This should be my motto through life. To love in suffering and to suffer in loving! Can there be a greater joy for a loving heart? Can love perhaps need rest, when its rest consists in never having rest?

Why, then, are you sad, O my soul, and why are you troubled at your weaknesses? Hope in God! Raise your eyes beyond the things of the earth, and confiding in the Mother of Holy Hope, remember the words: «Here below the cross, but afterwards, Heaven!»

O Mary, who passed your life on the cross and who now reigns in heaven, help us to have courage when the sorrows which pass seem overwhelming, in order that we may enjoy with you and Jesus the joys that never pass!

Amen.

34. SLAVE AND VICTIM

O, how these two words make me tremble with feeling!

Slave of God and of man, bound willingly with the chains of love and suffering. This is the part I must play, O Jesus, here in this holy house, basking in the warmth of your adorable presence.

Here I am, not to be served but to serve. Here I must aspire always to be the least and to be of no account in anything. What joy, and how my heart is transported with rapture at this idea, Jesus, God of my soul!

I am your slave. For a slave there is nothing but work, and pain and sorrow. But, alas, I do not deserve these precious pearls. Am I worthy of being a slave and victim?

No, certainly not. But I deeply desire to attain that supernatural poverty, that detachment from self, that self-abasement, and to have no wishes at all except for mortification and suffering.

Grant me the grace, O Jesus, to live far from myself and very near to you: to you, my Jesus, as a slave of love, held captive to the altar. Live in me, O my Jesus, Victim of love. Teach me and help me to sacrifice myself for you.

I wish my soul to be totally yours. I wish that my soul should animate my body solely that I may suffer.

I beg and implore you in your great goodness to grant me a complete detachment from and renouncement of self. For it is self that constitutes the real slavery. Give me complete annihilation of the old Adam, so that I may at last become a mere nothingness in favor, if I may say so, of God himself and of man.

Live your own life in me, my Jesus. A life of abasement and humiliation! Reduce my body and my heart to slavery so that I may always be the lowest of all.

But listen to me, Lord. I have another ambition, and that is not to remain at the same level of slavery which I offer you today, but to always go on at every moment diminishing, renouncing my own will, my thirst for affection, that human desire to please, that self-love, that anxiety to attract attention, with an ever increasing desire for self-annihilation.

Tear out and destroy all that is earthly in my heart so that the void may be filled with the Holy of Holies, the Victim of victims, who always abased himself and died thirsting to abase himself and to suffer more and more!

O Jesus, my soul's beloved! I promise to quench your thirst by continuing my life of voluntary crucifixion, for it is the ardent desire of your Divine Heart that until death I should be your slave and victim, for love of you.

O Mary, beloved Mother, perfect model for the slaves and victims of Jesus, help us to imitate your dear Son, the Divine Victim, in crucifying ourselves constantly for love of him!

Amen.

35. I WISH TO SUFFER

O yes, my Beloved, I wish to suffer! My heart beats with unusual violence on hearing these words, so that it vibrates with holy joy.

I wish to suffer in my soul, in my heart, in my senses and in all my faculties. But where shall I find a sufficiency of suffering to satisfy me? For that I must have recourse to you and ask you to answer the prayer of my wretched heart!

I wish to suffer in order to expiate my innumerable sins. I wish to suffer in thanksgiving for so many benefits received. I wish to suffer for poor abandoned sinners . . . for those who are ungrateful, for those to whom suffering is repulsive and who flee from it. For them I wish to suffer with all my soul, O my God!

I wish to suffer, in union with the merits of Jesus, in order to purchase heaven with the coin of suffering, the only coin which is current in the Divine market.

I wish to suffer with those who are at the point of death, with unbelievers, criminals, convicts . . . in order to hold back those who are on the point of falling into Hell, O my Eucharistic Jesus.

I wish to suffer for the souls in Purgatory . . . for the living . . . for the dead . . . for the just and for the depraved.

Hear me, O my Beloved, and incline your ear unto me!

Look, my Jesus, and see how ardently my whole being longs for suffering. And why? Why do you think that I wish to suffer? For your sake alone . . . in order to be like unto you, crucified, and because I love you with an intimate, ineffable, detached, ardent and burning love!

I wish to suffer because I know that in so doing I shall please you, and to give you pleasure is the sole desire of my life.

I love you not only in the Holy Eucharist, but also on Mount Calvary, for your love is in its very core connected with pain. I love you with a crucified love, in the thorns and the Cross, earnestly desiring the nails to attach myself to you, as the blind man earnestly desires the light, the miser gold; as he who is thirsty, the cooling spring.

How can I dread what to me is my life! O Jesus! My Jesus! Grant me to suffer unceasingly, so that full of enthusiasm for the Cross, I may open out to it my arms and my heart, in order to welcome it. Do not refuse me your caresses, those precious caresses which are your insults, your thorns, your tears and your Cross!

Yes, I wish to suffer, and that you should crucify me, should fasten me to the cross, for I hunger after the sweetness of Calvary, for that divine honey distilled from your cross.

O Mary, who by your sufferings merited the title of Queen of Martyrs, obtain for me the grace not to pass a single moment of my life without suffering something for the love of Jesus!

Amen.

36. «LEARN FROM ME, BECAUSE I AM MEEK AND HUMBLE OF HEART!»

Never did the Divine lips of Jesus say: «Learn from me that I am almighty, eternal, wisdom itself, that I am great, etc. etc.» Only on one occasion did he speak of himself and say, «Learn from me for I am meek and humble of heart».

O Jesus, most enchanting, most beautiful of the sons of men! O most gentle, most amiable Master of my soul! What gentleness, what sweetness, what humility and charity do I contemplate in your whole Being!

How much would I love to imitate you, O Jesus, and stop giving rude answers, or showing bitterness in my conversation, or roughness in my speech, and giving up any tone of superiority in talking to others.

Humility and meekness! How necessary are these Divine virtues in our daily communication with one another!

O Jesus! I stretch out my hands to you and beg you, in your great charity, to give me the virtues of gentleness and patience which I greatly need in order to resemble you.

Tell me, my beloved Jesus, tell me, O Lamb most gentle, the means you employed to endear so many hearts to you and win them for heaven?

— I will explain to you, my son, the way to win souls, so that you may learn from me and imitate me. It was, first of all, in practicing what I taught, that I attracted them to God. I never exaggerated the importance of those faults which were due not to malice, but usually to inexperience or to inculpable ignorance. I may say that I studied the different characters and adapted myself to them, leaving the grace of the Holy Spirit to act in them more or less slowly.

I won souls more easily by gentleness of speech than by bitter reproaches.

No one detests his sins until he receives Divine enlightenment from above and is inflamed with a burning love of God. To desire to act before he receives this help from above is like attempting to beat iron while it is cold, or wishing to tear him away by force from all that he holds dear.

He sees his faults much better who considers the beauties of virtue set before his eyes, rather than the ugliness of the defects alleged of him. It is in this way that the wounds of the soul are healed by meekness and patience. Never show annoyance towards those under your direction. It would be a serious error to insist upon all being equally perfect.

Shut your eyes to the weaknesses of the beginner. Come to his assistance and fortify him with good advice.

Never find fault with your brother in public, and never take advantage of his kindness.

Remember, my son, that people are won over more by honey than by vinegar.

Never lay the blame for anything on your neighbor but rather on yourself.

Derive from your prayers and meditations the gentleness which will make your heart like unto mine.

Remember that if I am thrice holy, I am likewise a thousand times Father, to forget, to pardon, and to receive with caresses all those who come into my arms.

— O my good Jesus, I thank you with all my heart for these precious counsels! Give me that Divine tact, that sweetness, and that humility and meekness of heart, so that I may love you as you love me, in order that I may know how to bear with others as you have borne with me.

O Mary, who better than you practiced the saying of Jesus, «Learn from me because I am meek and humble of heart?» Grant that always, and everywhere, we may be meek and humble of heart, we who love you so much, you and your Jesus!

Amen.

37. «DO YOU LOVE ME MORE THAN THESE?»

What can I answer you, Lord, you who see all the way to the bottom of my heart?

Ah yes, I want to love you more, if I possessed them, than all creatures in heaven and earth, more than all the angels and saints, more, yes, far more than a thousand worlds, and a thousand heavens! How can we not wish to love you immeasurably, O God of Love?

«Charity embraces in itself all the virtues», says St. Augustine. It represents faith, when we believe; hope when we are confident; strength, when we are victorious; patience, when we suffer in silence; mercy, when we have compassion on our neighbors; generosity, when we do good;

humility, when we abase ourselves; justice, when we give to every man his due. Indeed, charity includes all the virtues.

With love nothing is impossible; it undertakes all things, is first in all things, triumphs over all things.

«Of all strong things love is the strongest, of all sweet things, love is the sweetest».

Who would not ardently long for this love of God?

O Jesus, give me this love, this consuming fire, and make my heart ever beat in unison with yours! It will be this way when my gaze will always be on the sacred Host, when it will be continually fixed on you, without, however, my ever neglecting, even in the smallest detail, my daily duties on earth. O Jesus, yes, my heart ought to beat always in unison with yours, for you are my treasure and the only object of my life.

O yes, my Jesus, I want to love you more than all those who surround me, although in everything else I place myself beneath them.

I know my Lord, that in your eyes the degree of perfection to which we may attain is in direct proportion to the degree of love, to the interior beauty, to the purity and brilliance of that hidden sanctuary which is the innermost recess of the soul. It is there that the mysteries of the life of the heart are celebrated with God. That is the love I long for. I wish to have that purity of soul, that inward beauty which is so pleasing to you.

I wish to love you with humility, purity and all virtues, and also by crucifying and dying to myself.

«Who can battle against God?» said St. Bernard, «unless he makes use of the arms of love?» Ah, then, I long to battle with you, my Lord; and I shall triumph, for you yourself do offer me the arms for the combat, and do promise me the victory. How marvelous a thing is love!

O, yes, Mary, my good mother, what a marvelous thing is love, and who has ever understood it better than you? Make the love of Jesus to grow in us, and grant that it may be a love that suffers, a love like his and yours!

Amen.

38. AT MIDDAY

When before this time I have not lost sight for a moment of the Sun of my soul, this is the hour when I feel myself immersed in the plenitude of his love, impregnated and steeped in his Divine light and magnificence.

Jesus of my soul, since dawn my soul seeks for you, and like the flower that turns with the sun my gaze follows you, as do my thoughts, my desires, my sacrifices and my love!

I do not lose sight of you, my Jesus, my beloved Jesus, in my humiliations and in my little victories over self! The eyes of my body and of my soul do not turn away for an instant from their Eucharistic Sun, whose beneficent rays penetrate to all places with their dazzling brightness!

I receive you into my heart in the morning, O my Beloved, and in me you create a very ardent furnace of love, which goes on increasing in intensity until the happy hour arrives when I come to your Tabernacle to talk to you.

That hour is above all other hours the hour of love. Therefore my heart prefers it to all others. It is the hour of light and of grace, the hour when my heart overflows with enthusiasm, the hour of restrained tenderness, of suppressed ecstasy.

O my Jesus, my only love! Is there any hour when one cannot love you truly, earnestly, fervently? And yet it seems to me that the middle of the day lends itself more to the manifestations of love, here at the foot of this altar, beneath your gaze and your smiles, my hidden Jesus, who has shut yourself up in this sacrament for love you me.

This seems to be the hour when you are asking me for consolation. It seems to me to be the time to perform my enviable mission to you, my beloved Lord!

I understand that at this hour you would rest your eyes by looking at those lilies in the garden you have chosen . . . Your look seems to tell me to tear out the thorns from your Heart and to bury them in mine . . .

It seems to me that you asked for those ripe fruits of virtue in order to inhale their perfume . . . that you invited me into the shadow of your Cross to refresh the ardor of my soul; that you would repose on my breast, and in my heart. And why not, since in spite of my many miseries I open my arms to you in love?

O Jesus, my Beloved, chosen among a thousand, come to me, for I am dying of love for You!

Midday . . . O Mary, it is the sacred hour when every day I think of your sufferings . . . the hour when Jesus was nailed to the Cross in your presence; the hour of anguish when a double agony commenced, yours and his! O Mary, in beginning these three hours of love, make our hearts to be intimately united at the foot of the Cross and with the same object!

Amen.

39. «HE WHOM YOU LOVE IS SICK»

O Divine Physician, I come to knock at the door of your most tender heart. I come to say to you, «Lord, he whom you love is sick», and wishes to be healed. Therefore he comes to you, imploring your protection: say but the word, and my soul shall be healed.

My Jesus, see how weak I am in the face of my enemies! Help me in my battles against the world, against my own frivolity, lukewarmness, weariness, and laziness in your service.

Help me, Lord, for without you I can do nothing. I am good for nothing, not even to pronounce your Holy name as I should.

You, Lord, who has put this confidence in my heart, come to heal my wounds. O come, my beloved Father!

Should I ever become lukewarm in your service (never permit this, Lord!) I will fly to you, my Divine Savior, and you will revive my fervor with the fire of your Divine love. Should an exaggerated timidity ever invade my soul, I will fly to you, and you will restore my courage. If I were badly tempted to forsake you, I would fly to you in all humility, and you would carry me victoriously through all temptation.

If ever I should begin, unfortunately, to grow cold or lukewarm in your service, I would draw near to that Divine fire which inflames all hearts with good will.

If I begin to grow faint, I will eat the Bread of the strong, to restore anew my strength, and to make me keep my resolutions.

In this way I will cure the sickness of my soul and I will be healed beneath the beneficent shadow of the Cross.

Heal, Lord, the leprosy of my sins, the infirmities which defile my soul. You are my Father, and if you are my Father, and you will, you can heal me. I know that you love me, and how can you do anything else but cure me?

Pride overwhelms me. Impatience devours me. Frivolity overtakes me. Envy knocks at my door. Favoritism disturbs me. Contempt tortures me. Imagination carries me away. Work tires me. Despondency assails me.

What shall I do, O my hidden Jesus? To encourage my poor heart in its efforts, give me patience and a firm hope of victory.

Sorrow invades my soul. Routine undermines my purity of intention. Lack of confidence seeks to shake my vocation. Doubts obscure my mind and a thousand temptations assail me, forcing me to breathe a poisoned atmosphere which suffocates me.

What can I do, my Jesus? I can have recourse to you, through Mary's intercession, and prostrate at the foot of your throne, repeat with loving confidence in the presence of the Sacred Host: Lord, have pity on me, for he whom you love is sick!

Amen.

40. THE HOST

Can the soul explain what a consecrated Host is, what it feels on seeing Jesus in this hidden manner, and when approaching him in the Host, and what is the sensation produced by Divine contact with him in Holy Communion?

Who can see you, O Sacred Host, without being moved? Who is not attracted by your Divine beauty? Who on feeling your burning rays does not feel your warmth, and drink of the fountain of life?

Who does not feel his faith, his hope and his love increase in the presence of your incomprehensible abasement?

Who can contemplate you and not repent of his sins. I believe that if there were no consecrated Hosts in the world, I would have no difficulty in sacrificing the sight of my eyes. For the only real, ardent and profound desire I have is to see you, you alone, my Jesus! I place all my happiness in looking at you! Three times as happy as now would be he who could pass his life in doing nothing else but looking at you!

O Sacred Host, I carry your image engraved in my memory, but far more in my heart. I always seek you in the Ciborium, in the Tabernacle, in the Monstrance, as my eyes and my thoughts pierce brick walls, silk, precious metals, and even the appearance of bread which hides you, my Jesus.

I desire that as long as I live nothing would ever withdraw me from your benevolent influence; that no creature, no object of the world, would ever erase your memory. I beg you, O my Jesus, to grant that at the hour of my death the image of the Host may be engraved on my heart.

O my Jesus, who now hears me, I wish my last glance to be on you in the Sacred Host, and until that hour comes, never let my eyes be withdrawn from the Host or from the Cross.

Amen.

41. TO BE LESS

To be more, that is easy to understand, for our corrupt nature always seeks to rise, to exalt itself at all costs, to surpass our neighbors, to rule, to see our caprices, our self-love and our sensuality triumph.

But to be less, what does that mean? How is this science to be acquired? Where and in what book is it to be studied?

— In the Tabernacle, my son, at the foot of the altar, in the presence of the Host.

To be less is to free ourselves from all that we have in excess. It is, day by day, to get rid of all the imperfections that impede our progress, and to make a void in our hearts so that Jesus may fill it entirely with himself.

We must not only descend to the level of the dust trampled under foot by the passerby; we must not only hide ourselves and become slaves of God and of men, all the while in this state of abasement and abandonment still retaining mastery over ourselves; but it is necessary that we should disappear, if it were possible, from our own eyes and ardently desire to be pure, to be poor, to be a saint.

Who, in contact with your brilliant light, would not acquire a lily-white purity?

Who would not burn with a celestial fire on, even for a moment, thinking of your incredible love? Who could remain cold and indifferent, for an instant, in contemplating the marvels of the Holy Eucharist?

O my Beloved! O Lamb of God, who takes away the sins of the world! I approach you and I wish to be humble. I look at you and I wish to be mortified, penitent, to renounce myself, to be a martyr on the Cross.

I cannot be a moment at your feet without wishing also to be like you, a host, a victim, humiliated and despised.

When I raise my eyes to you, O pure, consecrated Host, I blush for very shame, and often I feel constrained to lower them again when I think of the impurity of my heart.

At other times, Lord, it is enough for me to approach you for the rays of your light to penetrate to the bottom of my soul and show it its misery and nothingness.

I gather untold riches from one single look at you, O Immaculate Host!

I know not what there is within that sacred white Host which lies there shining in the heart of the monstrance. Or rather, yes, I do know. It contains the living magnet. It contains Jesus. It contains Heaven!

O Star of the World, O Divine Sun, who makes all virtues spring up in our souls, who sows crosses and reaps lilies, why do I not love you as much as you deserve? It would be necessary for me to be another God in order to love you as the other Persons of the Blessed Trinity love you and as you deserve!

On seeing you, O Divine Host, I cannot but rejoice, even when my heart is breaking and my eyes are bathed in tears. I seem to see you through my tears, more beautiful, more transparent, more luminous.

There exists a special affinity between sacrifice and a consecrated Host, and the soul seems to realize the necessity of being a Victim in the presence of the Victim of victims, and of holy purity in the presence of Purity itself! My eyes recognize you, and on seeking you they find you, and realize the unfathomable depth of our misery and of our nothingness!

O Jesus, most humble Lamb of the Eucharist, enlighten me, send into my heart, O Light of Light, a ray of Your Glory and make me understand and practice that ideal of how to be less, for which my soul thirsts. Speak, my Jesus, for your poor servant listens!

— My son, you shall be less every time that you shall mortify yourself for love of me and for the good of your neighbors, always provided that you have obtained permission from your director to perform these acts of penance.

You shall be less if by constant self-denial you conquer your own will, if you continue to weaken the old Adam, to thwart your passions by mortification and self mastery and to renounce yourself for the Glory of God and the Salvation of Souls.

My son, if you desire other souls to become perfect, you must make yourself little, and humble yourself for love of them.

One can only give one's life for others by offering one's own life. And if you, by your zeal, will give yourself for your neighbors, you must tear your heart and your soul to pieces and give them away, so to speak, so that you must yourself disappear and I alone appear in your soul, attracting and reigning over the hearts of others.

Those who communicate life to souls must always be less in their own eyes; they must be ready at every moment to sacrifice their aspirations, their desires and their own will. They must never knowingly work for their own satisfaction.

They must labor to make their own personality disappear so that the saying of St. Paul may be manifested in them: «I live: now not I, but Christ lives in me».

— O my Lord, O most Divine Master of my poor soul, give me an ardent desire to be less, to descend, to diminish, to dissolve into my nothingness, so that you alone, my Jesus, may reign in me. Give life to other souls, even should it be necessary to take away mine. O Jesus, Jesus, take yourself the place that I occupy in the hearts of others.

Help me, Mary, O Beloved Mother, to become less, so that others may be more, and your Jesus may be glorified.

Amen.

42. HIS PLEASURE

Your pleasure is mine, O my adorable Jesus, for what can my soul, my intelligence, and my heart desire but what is pleasing to you and what you yourself desire?

O Jesus, my only love, my only joy, I rejoice today in renewing, at the foot of your altar, the unconditional offering of my desires, uniting them to yours forever.

But what was your pleasure, O love of all my loves, when you were here upon earth? Your pleasure was the Cross and can I allow You to get to Calvary without me? Give me that Cross, dear Lord. Give me a thousand crosses, or, if I must pass my life without devoting it entirely to suffering for you, make me perish in this very instant by the fire of your love.

O my Lord, I do not deserve this favor that every hour of my life should be marked with crosses, borne for love of you; but your generosity can give them to me and with them the strength to fight against nature and carry them with joy.

My Jesus, I know that you never refuse your grace to those whom you crucify. I know that those who follow you, walking in your footsteps, receive special graces and enjoy the feeling of being in your presence.

I know that they who are nailed to the cross with you, ever walk in the light, full of courage and enthusiasm because they are never separated from you.

Love attracts and draws to the Cross. It is the powerful magnet which makes the soul reach Calvary full of joy in spite of every obstacle. What other fuel except the Cross feeds this Divine fire? How can I consider my labors to be too heavy? How can I flee from every little pain?

O Jesus of my soul! If it be your pleasure that I should suffer from dryness, sickness, all kinds of troubles and tribulations, should this not be my pleasure also?

Ah, yes, for he who will not take up his cross and follow you is not worthy of you. I want to follow in your footsteps and be nailed to the same cross with the same nails.

My wretched body suffers in its pain; blind and sinful it shuns and abhors the Cross. But you, Lord, can strengthen my weakness and inspire in me an ardent love of sacrifice. You can help me to carry the Cross, and not only make it lighter, but enable me to arrive at Calvary sooner.

If I fall, you will help me to rise that I may continue to follow you on the road of suffering. O, my Jesus, give me a special love of the Cross so that there may be no other joy for me in the world except to live and die in its sweet embrace.

O my Beloved, if it was your pleasure to humble yourself, I ask you to humble me also. If it was your pleasure to crucify yourself, I ask you to crucify me. Put on my shoulders the white robe of Herod and the scarlet cloak of the soldiers: those two garments of humiliation and suffering which you wore. I wish to become like you and to engrave in my innermost soul the image of all your virtues.

Grant me the grace never to lose sight of you, that your will may always be mine, and your Cross, my Cross.

O Mary, whose joy when on earth was always to be humbled, forgotten, despised and crucified, ask Jesus to grant to each one of your children who live in these Houses of love and sacrifice, that your desires may always be ours, your inclinations always be ours, your pleasures ours, now and at every moment of our lives!

Amen.

43. HE AND I

Who can ever meditate enough on these words which teach us what God is and what we ourselves are . . .

He is everything . . . I am nothing. He is holiness; I am sin. He is tenderness and I am ingratitude. He is beautiful and I am mire, dirt and filth! And in spite of the infinite distance which separates us, he wishes me to love him, to unite myself to him, to identify myself with him, and that my heart may be transformed into his.

And with this goodness which confounds me, he is all in all to me. He superabundantly fills up all the emptiness of my soul, he draws all my affections, desires, aspirations and hopes. He is my food, my life, the air that I breathe, my haven of rest, my happiness, my all!

He is my only thought, my memory, my Paradise, my Heaven on earth! He is my Eucharist, my ideal, my very breath, my food and my drink! He is melodious music to me, sweetness itself, the nectar and scent of my soul, my strength, my delight, my measure, my desire! He calls forth my love in deifying me. He gives me life while taking it away. He sets my heart on fire, inflaming it with his glances . . . his beauty . . . his smiles . . . his love.

My hours and my minutes are his. My cradle is his and my tomb will acknowledge no other Master.

My troubles and my consolations, my sighs and my tears, my sorrows and my joys, all these are yours, my love, my Jesus, my God, three times Holy and a thousand times Father!

Lost, plunged, immersed in him, I live in him as a speck in the infinite. My life comes from God and to him it returns. He is my first beginning and my last end. I come from him and I go to him! O Jesus, how long?

Jesus waits for me with open arms on the cross and shows me his heart, the victim of my ingratitude. He shows me a crown on the summit of Calvary to which he calls me to climb, to crucify myself and to die with him for sinners. He goes before me, leaving me to follow in his blood-stained footsteps, and says: «Follow me, take up your cross and be poor, obedient and pure. Humiliate yourself, my son, and never exalt yourself».

He asks that I spend all my energy in his service, in order to renew it in heaven! He wants me to efface myself so that he may shine, that I should disappear, so that he may reign.

He teaches me that the last shall be first. He reminds me that I came to serve and not to be served, and that I am nothing and have nothing.

I can do nothing, I am worth nothing. I merit nothing, and his Divine teachings bring peace to my heart.

He makes me see clearly how great a favor it is that I am not in hell. He shows me how to hide myself in the depths of my nothingness, and that I am nothing but dust and ashes which the least gust of wind will scatter. He shows me that being what I am, of myself I am able only to offend him and be lost.

O what an unfathomable grace it is to know oneself! How closely I press this knowledge to my heart, for fear it should be taken away from me! Who has given me this pearl of great price? He alone, he who has lifted me above myself by love, and who calls me to a constant sacrifice with him on the Cross.

It is he who instructs me in the Science of the Cross by his example and makes me say with St. Paul: God forbid that I should glory except in the Cross of Our Lord Jesus Christ; by whom the world is crucified to me, and I to the world!

And Jesus, opening his arms, and still more his heart, makes me repeat with enthusiasm these words: «O Crux, ave, spes unica, amplius Domine!» More suffering, more sacrifices.

O my Jesus, chosen among a thousand, white and ruddy, holy and perfect, you are the plenitude of Beauty, of Power, of Goodness! You are the most tender Son, the most loving Father, the most affectionate Brother, the most faithful Spouse!

You are the quintessence of all charms, enchantment itself, the Word made Flesh, who charms the angels and is the wonder of the heavens; who gives joy to the Father and the Holy Spirit, who raises up Mary to the most sublime heights!

You are the Son of the incomparable Virgin, Lily of Lilies, dazzling ray of the Eternal Light.

He is He Who Is, and I could never be able to enumerate all his Divine qualities.

O my God! What is there that is beautiful, Divine and holy that is not he? It is right that my heart should overflow with love, attracted as it is by this powerful magnet which keeps it absorbed in itself, penetrating it through and through with love for him who is Love itself!

And now what shall I say of myself? I would rather not say a word, Lord, but would rather continue to proclaim what you are, for all that I have said is but a shadow, it is nothing compared to what you are. In the bottom of my heart you remain what you are, yes indeed. But to explain it is impossible, for no language exists which can express it.

I have given a slight sketch of what he is. But what am I? What can I say of myself? A mass of self-love, egoism, pride, vices and evil passions? It is enough to say that I am prone to evil, infidelity itself, weakness and corruption.

O my Jesus, here present, who hears me. How can you unite yourself to this mass of corruption, descend to it, attract this wretch to yourself, take it in your arms, pardon it and not disdain to love it?

Of my most gentle Savior, what a contrast, you and I! You must indeed be God to tolerate me!

In those two letters, He, are contained my past, my present, my future, my heaven! And in that other letter I is to be found the heaviest cross for my most loving Jesus.

What a disgrace! He and I!

O Mary, my Mother, I do not forget that you are between him and me, because at Bethlehem you gave me Jesus, and at the foot of the Cross you remained standing between Jesus and me and all miserable sinners. O Mother, draw the bonds of union between him and me ever closer, a union of love and suffering on earth, of love and of glory with you in Heaven!

Amen.

44. LIFE CONSISTS IN KNOWING YOU

Ah yes, Life of my life, life consists in knowing you, for whoever knows you, cannot do less than love you even to the point of delirium, even to martyrdom!

I am painfully afflicted when I think of the bitter complaint which came one day from your heart: «After I have been with you all this time you still do not know me, Philip?»

I apply these words to myself, my Jesus. I suffer, I weep. I would live that true life which consists in knowing You and despising myself.

All that is not you is death, and how then can he have life who does not know you?

But how am I to know you, my Beloved Jesus? By remaining constantly in your sweet presence, by thinking of you . . . leading a life of respectful intimacy and confidence, a life of prayer and meditation.

To know you is to be pure of soul and chaste of body, like St. John, who, before anyone recognized you said with emotion: «It is the Lord!» He, the Virgin Apostle, felt and divined your presence with the purity of his soul. This is an important point, absolutely necessary in order to discover your presence even in the darkness of the obscure night of the spirit.

My Jesus, without seeing you yet feeling your presence, how often does one exclaim: «It is the Lord!» He who is pure in soul divines and feels your illuminating presence from afar. It matters not that the darkness of night surrounds you. He knows and feels beneath the veil of the sacramental elements your warmth, your breath, your respiration, your scent, your glances, your caresses, and your heart. «It is the Lord!» he says. he knows you because he possesses the life of grace and of love, the life of purity, and, therefore, thanks to his purity, he is allowed to see God even in this life, like the saints do.

Yes, Jesus, pure souls know you and in knowing you, they love you, and in loving you they possess the true life which has no end, because to know you is to have life.

And, therefore, O my Jesus, I beg you to engrave your Divine image on my heart profoundly and forever.

But if life consists in knowing you, it is because in knowing you one cannot do less than imitate you, crucifying oneself and imbedding in the soul your thorns, your nails and your Cross!

Come then to my arms, O my Jesus! Come into my mind and into my heart, in order to form of me a living Cross from which you will never more separate yourself.

Who can know you better than the Cross? Therefore the Cross has life, I wish to resemble it and like an ivy attach myself to your Body, to your Soul, to your Heart, and perceive your divine glances, your smiles, your wishes, and then fly to execute them.

Amen.

45. WHEN THERE IS LOVE!

Yes, my adorable Jesus, when there is love, there is all! Therefore I come today to beg of you with all my soul to give me love to love you, for I am dying with a desire to love you more and more.

I ask you, Lord, to give me a heart of fire, a heart which says: «To love, Lord, or to die». «Not to die but to suffer». «Always to suffer more». «To love and to be despised for your sake».

Give me a heart, O Jesus, that does not count the number of its sacrifices nor the extent of its love.

Where there is love, all obstacles disappear. There are no mountains so high that they cannot be crossed, no burning fiery coals too hot to be trampled on . . .

When there is love, thorns are turned into roses and crosses into pearls.

When there is love, suffering is the indispensable food for the soul, contemptuous treatment is an honor, humiliations are crowns, and the follies of the Cross treasures.

O my good Jesus, source of all love, where are you? Lord Jesus, come and fill up the depths of my soul with love.

Whom shall I follow, if not you?

Whom shall I seek but you?

Whom shall I love, if I do not love you?

O Jesus, you alone can strengthen my weakness, dispel my ignorance, heal my wounds and change tepidity into fervor.

Who could it be who would have always loved you? who could it be that has never offended you? Who would have separated himself from you?

Give me, Lord, that perfect detachment from all that is not you. Give me that pure love which will cause me to give up all inordinate affections, and which will prefer your friendship to all others. Give me a pure heart, detached from everything, and with no other desire but to do your will.

O my Jesus, my only love! I am going to ask you today for a great grace: it is not only to prefer your will to everything else, but also to have that holy detachment which goes further still, and which loves nothing but to love for your will.

Give me a heart, Lord, that does not choose, but is always ready for anything, only desirous of doing your will; a heart that does not attach itself to the things God wants, but to the will of God who determines them. This is a lofty ideal. I know it, my Jesus, but when there is love, the heart is filled with the most sublime aspirations, with irrepressible zeal and fiery ardor, with a thirst for purity, a hunger for martyrdom, endless crosses and an unlimited confidence in God.

Give me then, O Jesus, your love, an ardent love which consumes all that is not Divine. Shall I not say with St. Augustine: «Why cannot I make use of an infinite love in order to love an infinite love?»

To love, and to sacrifice myself like Mary! To crucify myself for you. Such will be my constant ideal, until I possess you eternally in heaven.

Amen.

46. HE OR I?

One or the other must reign in my soul. If he enters, I must at once retire, and if it is I who enter, it is he who must withdraw, for it is certain that Jesus will not dwell in a heart that is already inhabited. And yet when creatures are the guests in the heart, he chooses sometimes himself to make them retire. But when there is pride, self-love and egoism, he leaves that dwelling, and the Holy Spirit cannot enter into it.

How delicate is the Lord with the souls he wishes to possess! When he operates in a soul to sanctify it, he empties it of itself and drives out all creatures and inanimate things as well. In a word, he renders it simple. The Lord does not like complicated things, nor even an exaggerated variety of pious practices. He desires the heart to be completely empty so that he alone may occupy it.

If the soul yields itself to this operation and remains constantly faithful, then the inspirations of grace that it will receive will be more numerous and more pressing.

If the desire for self-sacrifice and for advancement in the things of God is feeble, the inspirations of grace will be less urgent and less strong. But if the soul wishes, no matter what the price, to reach the summit of love, it will receive the necessary light and the most pressing impulses, for the more the soul gives to God the more exacting will be he. And he will permit the trials to increase, so that the number of victories may be more numerous.

The Lord will subject that soul to new trials which will impose unforeseen sacrifices. He will reveal secret attachments, traces of self-love or lack of courage and generosity that were unknown before.

It is in this way that Jesus treats the souls of those who give him free scope for action and who, divesting themselves, proclaim him King of their hearts. But those who seek themselves, remain their own masters and envelope themselves with incense. He leaves them alone on the throne of their pride.

If he finds neither strength nor good will in souls he wishes to form, he makes no further attempt to purify them.

O my Jesus, my Heaven, my only Love! Do not let me occupy a place in my soul which belongs to you. I desire to renounce myself for love of you. Make me go out of myself forever, that you may enter, my good Lord, and entirely fill my heart.

May you alone be the end and aim of my desires, of my life. Let me seek you alone, go to you, follow you, approach you, love you, and have no other fear except to lose you.

Let it be you, and not I, who shall live and reign in my soul here and for all eternity!

O Mary, my Mother, bring me the grace that, in imitation of you, I may never think of myself but of Jesus only, to love him and imitate him in renouncing myself always!

Amen.

47. JESUS LOVED US FIRST

It was not I who chose you, my beloved Jesus, but it was you who from all eternity chose this wretched little earthworm.

You loved me first . . . and even before the sun had ever shown I was already in your thoughts. I had not yet come into the world, and yet your blood had already redeemed me.

I was yours, even before knowing you and loving you. And for how many graces, which literally overwhelm and astound me, do I have to thank you?

Hardly had I reached the age of discretion when I began to offend you. But you, who had loved me first, had already prepared a remedy for my faults in the Sacraments!

You washed me in the waters of Baptism. And, as often as I wished, you cleansed my soul of its impurities in the words of absolution.

How many Communions have I made when one alone would have been enough to have made me a Saint!

And your grace? How often have I misused this divine gift? And my Guardian Angel who has delivered me from so many perils! And the Mother of God who became my Mother! . . . And the Heart of Jesus and his unutterable love and unlimited tenderness! And the Giver who is truly more than the gift! . . . How can I be grateful enough for such great benefits, and for innumerable special and particular benefits, as well as for those that I shall certainly receive in the future?

O my God, how great is my ingratitude! I know not how to give the due response to that eternal love which has drawn me out of nothing, which has given me life, and has first loved me!

May every instant of my life, every moment of my existence, every beating of my heart, be consecrated to you for all future time!

I shall make a daily account of how I guard my senses, of how I use my time, and of the neglect and laxity which so sadly diminish my fervor.

I shall question myself as to the degree of fervor with which I make my meditations, hear Mass, receive holy Communion . . . how I prepare myself, and what fruits I derive from these.

I shall probe my soul to the very bottom, desirous as I am of getting a clear idea about what should be reformed, taken away, put in its place, ruthlessly torn away; and all with that generosity which love alone can give.

O Jesus, you who first loved me, help me to keep the following resolutions:

Outwardly:
1. Exact fidelity to my way of life.
2. To do everything well.
3. To be careful not to neglect little details.

Inwardly:
1. A great purity of intention.
2. Continual remembrance of the presence of God.
3. To do everything for love.

This is what I propose, in order to respond to the love of him who first loved me, O my beloved Jesus.

O Mary, I know that after Jesus no one has loved me, loves me or will ever love me as much as you have done, for you are my mother! I beseech you to obtain for me the grace to keep these holy resolutions so that I may more faithfully imitate you and Jesus.

Amen.

48. TO LOVE IS TO SUFFER

How true this is, my Jesus! There is no love without pain, no charity without sacrifice! To love is to suffer! And, in order to know how much one suffers, it is necessary to know how much one loves!

And this, you alone know, you alone, Master of my being. You alone, my Jesus hidden here within the Host, can measure the extent of my love. I wish that it were immeasurable! And if the Cross is the measure of your love for me, it is also with the Cross that I will measure my love for you.

What a marvelous and delightful measure! The Cross with its outstretched arms. The Cross, emblem of the love of God, price of eternal glory, the sign of salvation, the banner of my battles, the triumph of my victories!

If I bind myself to you, O most Holy Cross, perpetual companion of my soul, it is because I love Jesus who hears me. Death alone shall separate me from you; but the love that my heart proclaims for you will live and reign forever.

I honor you in the presence of my Master, O most Holy Cross, hidden Wisdom, unknown source of light, honor of those that serve you, safety of those who carry you, crown of those who bind themselves to you, reward of those who love you, salvation of those who place their whole trust in you!

O precious Cross, whoever dies on you shall live. Whoever dies in you and loves you is content. He who seeks you, finds you.

You ascend to heaven and you penetrate into hell. Your arms are never closed. they protect all men. You burn always with the fire of love for him who sacrificed himself on you. And to all who seek you and love you, you transmit this fire. You confound the world. You overthrow the proud. You crown the humble. And you fill the heavens with your chosen ones!

O my good Jesus. To love is to suffer and to suffer is to love! Never let me be deprived of suffering. Never let there be a single moment of my life without the cross at my side.

If I want to love you to delirium, I must be ready to suffer martyrdom! O Blessed Cross, who could ever shun you? Who could ever tear you out of his heart? Who will ever know your secrets? Who will ever be able to count the joys that are hidden in you? You do reanimate the souls of those who are led astray, cast down, suffering, persecuted, or in anguish.

You are the best friend of him you show the greatest severity. If you take away the good things of the earth, you give in exchange spiritual blessings. If your deprive us of natural human affections, you give us the love of God. If you let us be bombarded with insults, you give us the crown of glory. If you seem to abandon us, you unite us on the contrary to our God.

You deliver those whom you enchain. You absolve those whom you condemn. And to those who you deprive of everything, you give Jesus, the treasure of Heaven . . .

O Cross, beloved Cross. I accept all your pain in exchange for your divine love!

Amen.

49. «OBEDIENT UNTO DEATH»

The model of obedience for me is Jesus whose food and drink were to do the will of his heavenly Father. «My food is to do the will of him that sent me». This obedience crucifies him unceasingly, but this Cross, like all the others, was rendered light and sweet by love.

All the crosses of Jesus were due to his obedience. He obeyed by going to Bethlehem. He obeyed by his flight to Egypt. He obeyed by remaining in the Temple: Did you not know that I must be about my Father's business? For thirty years he lived in obedience to his parents, and his last words on the cross were: «It is finished». «Into your hands I commend my spirit», which obeyed you unto the very last.

«If you love me», said the Lord, «keep my commandments». This means that it is through disobedience that love is lost. He who does not love him will not keep his commandments.

Adam fell through disobedience. The blind and the proud who will not obey, will also fall, but the «obedient man shall sing of victory».

Disobedience proceeds from three sources: the first is self-approval, which blinds the soul and makes it ignore its natural baseness. This presumption caused the fall of Lucifer, whereas Mary was exalted by her incomparable humility.

The second source of disobedience is confidence in one's own judgment. The light often fails to penetrate those who are so blinded, and it has often been the cause of heresies.

The third source is a certain pride in abandoning God for the creature; being unwilling to disappoint others or even oneself and to deprive oneself of those things in which man seeks consolation. It was this disobedience that caused the fall of Adam. He would neither grieve his companion nor renounce himself.

O my Jesus hidden here within the Host. Incomparable model of obedience! Give me that virtue and the grace necessary to keep the following resolutions, seven pearls of great price which will sanctify me if I am able to keep them:

1. I will obey for the love of God; as if it were he himself who was speaking by the mouth of my superior, because it is certain that the voice of my superior, the voice of direction, is the voice of God.

2. I will obey promptly, without a moment's delay, and even anticipate the desires of my superior.

3. I will always obey, and make all my actions supernatural, even in eating, drinking, sleeping, etc., by doing them all for God.

4. I will obey with simplicity, blindly, without criticising inwardly or outwardly.

5. I will obey joyfully, without manifesting any repugnance, making continual efforts to appear always content.

6. I will obey like Jesus unto death so that his most sacred Will may be the support of my soul.

7. I will pray, I will work, I will strive to obtain the spirit and the perfect observance of this beloved virtue, by imitating Mary, the Queen of Obedience.

O Jesus, who hears me, give me the grace today to die to myself and to live in entire subjection to the will of others! Make me understand that obedience in act is the lowest form of obedience, that obedience in act and will is the most saintly, and that obedience in will, act and intelligence, is the most perfect.

O my God! It is said that few reach this state of perfection, but with the assistance of your grace you can make me become one of these chosen few, so that I may, in this way, do all the more for your glory.

Amen.

50. WITHOUT MEASURE

It is in this way that I would love you, my Jesus hidden here within the Host, without measure, with all the power of my heart, with all the energies of my soul.

Without measure in suffering . . . without measure in love.

I wish to love you without making those trivial calculations which nature demands, without the pettiness and meanness of a fickle heart. Give me today an unlimited generosity, that I may immolate at your feet all my affections, opinions and desires. I have offended you so much up till now. I have been so unfaithful and ungrateful to you, Light of my life, that I wish to weep for the time lost and to offer you a life all sacrifice and love.

How often have you, O Jesus, who now listen to me, cast your eyes at the same time as I did on the innumerable base actions I have committed? How often, Lord, have you offered me your love while I have given mine to creatures? You were always pursuing me and I have always shunned your Divine presence! You, Jesus of my soul, ever dwelling in me, and I ever far from you! O my only Master! Is it not true that my ingratitude to you and your love for me are both immeasurable?

O my Glory, my Treasure! I am filled with grief and sorrow when at once I contemplate your tenderness and the utter lack of delicacy of my wretched heart.

How often have you knocked at its door without my opening it? How often have you entered and I have rejected you? How often have I preferred the company of the creature to yours for the sake of some illicit pleasure or evil passion?

Ah, my Love, my Heaven, forgive me in your goodness and tear out this luke-warmness from my soul. You, Lord, who does not tolerate the cold heart, and who holds the lukewarm heart in abhorrence, yet have lived in this lukewarm heart. Tear it out, Lord. Change and transform this poor heart which would now be altogether yours!

From now on I will only breathe for you. Have pity on this miserable sinner and receive me into your Heart! Do not trust me, Lord, I who am meanness itself. That is my measure, but you, my Jesus, you alone are great in all things, in suffering, in loving, in concealing my faults, and in pardoning me. That is your measure, the measure of your mercy which is without measure. Ah, then, employ it in my favor, and make up with your love for my helplessness and nothingness!

You who are Almighty, inflame my heart, and make it burn with a heavenly fire which will heal all its wounds.

O my God, consume me with the fire of the Cross. I see you nailed to it, crowned with thorns, covered with blood, and I cannot restrain my emotion when I see you looking at me with a smile and with your arms outstretched, saying to me: Fear not, my son, this is the measure of my love. Weep and be thankful, for the measure of my love for you is the cross, and the Cross is immeasurable.

Amen.

51. MY HOUR OF HEAVEN

What can it be but this, my Jesus, my Treasure? It is my hour of adoration, during which, while kneeling in your presence, I look at you and you at me. It is the hour in which you bless me humbly prostrated at your feet. It should be called the «hour of love», for love is heaven, love is life, love is everything!

I come here, my Jesus, to open my heart to you and to display all its weaknesses. I come to talk to you and to hear your sweet voice. I come to take you in my arms and press you to my heart. I come to relate to you all the secret sorrows of a heart which adores you so tenderly. I come to you bathed in tears for love of you.

O Lamb of God, whiter than ermine! I come to you at this holy hour to cover you with the most tender and loving embraces, to feed on you, and to inhale your Divine presence.

My Life, Love of my soul, you know what I ask you, and what you answer, what I tell you about and what I promise you.

During this hour the world does not exist for me. Neither father, nor mother, nor relations, nor friends, nor anything else.

Only you and I, my Jesus here present with me! You and I uniting ourselves, identifying our souls, our hearts, our wills!

One thing only, during these precious minutes can accompany my love and that is pain. Pain to see you offended and so little loved. The pain caused by lack of zeal. The pain of not being an angel, a martyr. The pain of seeing so many souls going to perdition. And the thought of your love, beloved Jesus, increases this pain still more. This is why my heart is breaking, my Beloved. My torture augments, and I therefore ask your pardon and mercy a thousand times, while offering myself to undergo whatever sacrifice may be pleasing to you.

It is here, Lord, that you advise me. Here that you encourage me to follow in your footsteps and never to abandon the Cross. It is here that you strengthen me and forgive my sins!

O incomparable happiness! It is here that you remind me of my weaknesses, and teach me a remedy for them.

It is here that you open your heart to me, secure refuge for sinners, haven of rest for the weary, an oasis for those who are journeying through the desert of the world.

O loving Jesus, who loves when you were living, who loves when you were dying, who loves after your death, who loves eternally!

Death cannot exhaust your love. You have allowed your heart to be opened by a lance to let me see my name inscribed on it! Not even in death do you forget me, Lord, for you were careful to cause your side to be opened, in order that your Blood might flow from it to purify all things and in order that I might penetrate into the innermost recesses of that loving Heart where all the Divine treasures of your grace are accumulated.

This is what you do for me during my hour of adoration. You remind me of your blessings and you show me the Cross and exclaim: «Onward, my son, onward, even should you have to climb over a mountain of suffering, ascend the thorny path which leads to Calvary for love of me! If no one understands you, if you find no echo in other hearts, behold, here is mine which is all yours. Should any souls escape from you and follow another direction, pray, be silent, and offer yourself for them! In all your sorrows I am near you, although you may not feel my presence. Courage, life is short and heaven is eternal!»

This is what Jesus says to me during my hours of heaven, my sacred hours, my hours of love.

This is what Mary repeats to me. I always feel that she is near me during my hour of heaven, and I shall never leave her side so that I may love Jesus better in the school of his Divine Mother.

52. WHAT DO YOU SAY TO ME, LORD?

I say to you, my son, that I came down from Heaven because I saw you very far off and very lonely without me . . . because, poor little earthworm, my love for you impelled me to take your flesh and become man, in order to give you mine in this consecrated Host, to live near you and within you, to occupy the poor and silent shelter of the Tabernacle and of the hearts of men on earth.

I say to you, that if you have loved me for a few years, I have loved you from all eternity, and neither your sins, negligences, contempt or ingratitude have been able to chill my love for you.

I say to you, my beloved son, that my passion and my martyrdom did not suffice to quench my thirst for suffering, and that I wish you to continue to do what I can no longer do. That is to suffer in body and soul, becoming a victim in union with me, and that you should offer me and offer yourself at the same time for the realization of my projects of redemption.

I want simple, pure, humble, and generous souls who will place all their happiness in sacrificing themselves for me.

I say to you that I have instituted this sacrament in order to be more alone with you and nearer to you, while Heart beats against heart that I may in this way most clearly reveal to you what is my will, each moment.

I am here to see those who wish to approach me, to count their virtues, to compare their fervor, to suffer their neglect and console myself with their love.

I follow them with my eyes. Their names and their features are engraved in my heart. When I see them approaching me to obtain food and life at my feet, I distribute graces to them in abundance. I cover them with caresses, and I want to draw them nearer and nearer to him who is their Life by means of those perfect virtues of self-sacrifice, self-denial and voluntary mortification.

I say to you that I want from you greater purity of soul, greater humility, and greater forgetfulness of self.

My son, I want you to complete my Passion in your own flesh, by making yourself a victim in union with me. I want you to purchase purity for this corrupt world. I want you to crucify yourself, unseen and unknown, by means of that suffering which unites, sanctifies, and obtains graces; by means of those hidden renunciations which make me smile and disarm my heart, which is all tenderness and goodness; by those expiations which appease the justice of God and stay his hands when about to punish.

I wish that your heaven on earth should be to suffer for me; to become as the sacrificial wood which is burnt in honor of me and on behalf of those who offend me.

This is what your Jesus says to you, my beloved one, during these silent moments which nothing can disturb save the palpitation of my Heart and of yours which beat together in unison, and understand and love each other.

O Jesus, my beloved Lord and Master! I will keep your desires in my heart, grant me the grace to fulfill them!

O Mary, my good Mother, help me to do the will of my Jesus, for it is the wish of my heart to pass my life consoling him, and showing him how much I love him!

Amen.

53. MY THORN OF TODAY

You know what it is, my beloved Jesus. You alone know and measure the depth of suffering it causes me.

It pierces my heart and makes my whole being quiver at its contact. But no matter! I come to offer it to you with all my heart, and I would have it pierce even deeper, in order that I might have more suffering to offer you! For I know, my Jesus, that my sufferings alleviate yours, and that the thorns which pierce me rip out the ones on your forehead.

Is it not then unutterable joy for me to crown my heart and my head with thorns, since in piercing myself I can console you?

But there are so many kinds of thorns which come from God and from man!

There are some so cruel and so distressing that they undermine the soul and cause it inconsolable agony! There are the thorns of public humiliation, of scorned affection, discourteous refusal, unfounded suspicion. Above all, there are the thorns of ingratitude, and these are the most painful, the most piercing, because they are those that, alas, make your Heart bleed the most, O my beloved Jesus!

There are more thorns in the world than crosses, and I desire to love them, to kiss them, and to receive them, to press them against my heart.

The thorns are the myrrh which my poor soul ventures to offer to the Beloved One! They are roses for me, ah yes, because they are such for my Jesus!

My path is strewn with these precious flowers which never fade; and according to the amount of blood with which they are sprinkled, they increase and multiply and fill the soul with their Divine perfume.

That is why every morning I joyfully pluck the first thorn which springs up before me, and I offer it to you, Lord, watered with my tears, because this dew, this blood of the soul, purifies it and magnifies its beauty.

I offer it to you, and you, my good Jesus, you drive it into the most delicate fibres of my heart. In driving it in, you tear it out of your own, and at this I rejoice and only wish that I had millions more to offer to you.

O my Eucharistic Jesus, leave me not for a moment without those thorns which pierce me in body and soul! Be not sparing of these pearls with which I wish to be surrounded, only because I love you!

O Mary, your heart was pierced by thorns innumerable; make my heart like yours!

Amen.

54. «SAVE US OR WE PERISH»

Ah, yes, my Lord and my God, who is here present. The tempest rages in the bottom of my soul. Storms succeed storms unceasingly. The bitter waters of suffering come to my lips and have inundated my heart.

I feel lost, my Jesus, in the midst of these rising floods. Floods of pride, anger and jealousy, envy and spite! Save me, Jesus, awake and listen to me or I perish!

My faith is very languid, my hope seems dead, and charity no longer inflames my frozen heart. Save me, Lord, you who are my Savior!

See, Lord, what a miserable wretch I am, how wrapped up in self, so easily attaching myself to creatures, so touchy, so ready to find fault with others and so slow to correct my own faults! Save me from myself, for I fall so frequently, even without being tempted by the devil.

Obedience costs me dearly. Others being preferred to me hurts me. Effort tires me. And luke-warmness permeates me. Save me, my Jesus, for without your help I perish!

Flattery in some form is a necessity for me. I let myself be guided by my nerves and by passing impressions which leave my heart cold and empty.

Save me, my good Jesus, and hear me for your mercy's sake!

I feed on vain fantasies. Criticism is painful to me. I am a religious person only in name. O my Jesus, is this the same person who pretends to want to be one with you by being crucified?

Calm, then, the hurricane which threatens to shipwreck me and the tempest which is ready to engulf me!

Calm my temptations. Dissipate these black clouds which are about to burst over my head, my Jesus, and save me!

O Mary, star of the sea, pacify the heaven of my soul and say to my Jesus, Save him, save him, for he is my child and he is about to perish!

Amen.

55. INCENSE

Incense does not give out its perfume unless it falls on burning coals. I wish to be your incense, my beloved Jesus, even if I have to pass through the flames and submit to the tortures of martyrdom. Will you grant me this wish?

The soul is inflamed with the fire of love. This fire also burns and destroys by slowly consuming the heart, the body, the entire life, in honor of the Beloved. To suffer! What does it matter since the perfume that is pleasing to Jesus consists of suffering?

Ah, what infinite sweetness suffering brings to those souls that belong solely to God!

Incense! How beautiful is the word, and how symbolic! From my earliest childhood I have envied it, for when it burns, as it were, it ascends and envelops Jesus amidst its vapors and perfumes. It ascends continually and penetrates to the interior of the Tabernacle.

How sweet must death be to those who during life have been the incense of Jesus, and who have always lived on the Cross among the burning embers of his Divine love!

How beautiful does suffering appear to the soul which is inspired with love of the Eucharist!

If we could spend a moment in heaven, we would understand the value of a moment of suffering. Then we would not find any cross heavy enough, or any trial bitter enough.

O my Jesus, consume me like incense at the foot of your altar, by the fire of desolation, abandonment, humiliations and suffering!

I am your incense for my own happiness. I will ascend to your throne and envelop you like a cloud, and lovingly embrace you and screen you from the scrutiny of all who wish to disparage you! Most sacred Host, most beloved Tabernacle! You will be mine every time that my heart will burn like incense on the fiery embers of humilia-

tion and sacrifice; every time that I give up my
own will and renounce myself. Every time that I
suffer an affront in silence, that I conquer myself
and that I sacrifice myself for love of you.

Then I will be your incense when I shall surrender myself into the hands of obedience,
renouncing every wish of my own, and letting
myself be placed by God and man on the burning
embers of love and suffering.

Amen.

56. HEAL ME

Ah yes, my Jesus, my Divine Physician, heal
me for your mercy's sake.

Lord, you see how deep my wounds are,
and you know how dangerous they are!

Lord, he whom you love is sick. My Jesus, I
will tell you of my suffering that you may heal
me, and I will show you my leprosy that you may
cure me.

Pride and vanity are my most obdurate sins.
I cultivate useless affections, friendships which
obscure your presence in my soul even if they do
not altogether prevent my union with you.

I feel my self-love wounded. I feel pleased with myself. I am uncharitable towards others and indulge in rash judgments. I am very slow in responding to your inspirations. I do not mortify myself and do nothing to conquer myself.

I have to accuse myself of so many faults against silence and obedience; so many excuses and negligences in your service, such obstinacy, alas, in adhering to my own opinion.

How will I heal myself? How can I come to understand which is the most serious of the many infirmities which cause my soul to decay?

My Jesus, I will examine myself by the light of the Holy Eucharist during the hour of adoration that I pass at your feet, with my soul painfully wounded.

My Jesus, I am listening. Enlighten me and speak to my heart!

— Pay attention, my son. All your ills come from pride and from lack of recollection. In general, your soul is troubled when you are deprived of praise, affection, consideration. These ills also proceed from the fact that you seek the creature, not in order to be led to me, but to satisfy your self-love. And should you not succeed, you are disturbed and uneasy, searching for empty pleasures which can only leave a void in your heart.

My son, you do not seek me, but you seek yourself in others. And that is why you cannot find peace.

You will only find that peace on the day when, denying yourself, you are resolved with all your will to annihilate yourself in every way.

Make up your mind that in order to be happy it is only necessary for you to disappear . . . to come down, to detach yourself from yourself and to leave me full scope, for I alone can give you happiness in humiliation and suffering.

By this means only can the soul taste the holy joys of recollection and mortification which are its life. Only in this way can you remain in the presence of God and in union with him.

Humility: that is the remedy if you desire to be healed.

Lose sight of yourself. Be convinced of your own nothingness, my beloved son. Endeavour to be the least before men, and the greatest only before God.

O Mary, make us humble like yourself!

Amen.

57. «WITHOUT ME, YOU CAN DO NOTHING»

It is true, Lord! What can the disciple do without his Master? Of what value is the Cross without Jesus nailed on it?

My Jesus, without you I am a broken reed, a barren desert, stubble and chaff, only fit for the eternal fire.

Is it possible that Sisters of the Cross can ever be deprived of his most loving Master, of the only love of his soul? Is it possible that a living Cross can exist that does not bear on it Jesus living and breathing? My beloved Jesus, no one here wishes to be anything, or do anything of himself: everything with you and for you!

Those who wish to carry the Cross can only do so in union with you. Without you what can they do except fall into sin and be lost?

Without your aid they would sink deeper and deeper into the mire of their infirmities and imperfections.

When I, alas, have had the misfortune to offend you, Lord, it was always because I had thought myself capable of doing something without the assistance of your grace. How often vanity has sullied my actions. And how often the mirror of my soul, in which your image is reflected, has been tarnished by vain self-satisfaction.

How often, alas, (pardon me, O Jesus!) I formed resolutions without asking you in my prayers what were your plans; without humiliating myself to find the light; without remembering to consult you who are everything here!

In the midst of reproof and corrections, have I sought your assistance above all, your good will, and your favor? When I have made mistakes, in a thousand circumstances, was it not because of having counted solely on myself and forgetting that without you, who hears me, I can do absolutely nothing?

Who is it that gives being and life to all that exists? Is it, by chance, I? Who is the light of the World? Who can stir up our hearts? Who gives meaning to the letter? Who can make himself Master of our wills? Who but you, all powerful and Almighty God!

What is man without you? The word convinces, but the blood alone persuades, that is to say, the life of sacrifice in union with Jesus. Art makes the orator, but suffering alone makes the saint.

Words move us, but sanctity alone converts. In order to influence men effectively, it is first of all necessary to lean on God.

We can do nothing without Jesus, but with him we can do everything. «I can do all things in him who strengthens me».

Amen.

58. TO SEE JESUS IN EVERYTHING

Such should be the life of the sons of the Cross: to see Jesus in everything. Is it not so, my Jesus? To see you always working and directing everything for our greater good!

Lord, I come today to ask you through the intercession of Mary Immaculate, to grant my desire for the grace to live constantly in the presence of God in order to see you, to hear you, and to consult you in everything.

My beloved Jesus, may I constantly see your image in my superiors, as well as in my brethren!

«It is Jesus», I shall say whenever humiliations and difficulties present themselves. It is Jesus who comes to me hidden under these veils. It is the Lord, I shall repeat, when trials come to assail me. It is his visit in the form of a cross.

When I breathe the withering atmosphere of desolation, when through abandonment and desertion my soul grows faint and weary, «It is the Lord, it is Jesus», I will say, and I will press to my breaking heart all these sorrows and sufferings, these trials and struggles.

Oh, if in everything I could only have a supernatural vision to make me see the hand of God and his holy will in everything; a vision which would make me realize the presence of Jesus who hides himself to make me feel the contact of suffering through his love! Ah, then I would see in every trial a grace and in every contradiction a Divine favor!

How barren is this life without Jesus who, when we are by his side, makes every cross appear sweet! Why, then, Lord, do I suffer and weep? Is it not because I do not walk by faith, because I forget you, and fail to understand that you dispose all things for my welfare?

What is lacking in me, Lord, except to make my life a supernatural one and ever to keep you present in my thoughts, both in joys and sorrows, while repeating at every step with ardor: «It is the Lord!»

Jesus, give me that clear light of faith which will always enlighten me and which will enable me to see that it is you who come to me in sickness and in health, in suffering and in joy, for I wish to live in you, in your life, and according to your lovable will. Never fail to enlighten me with your presence, for you are my Light, and you are also he who puts to my lips the cup of bitterness.

Even should my heart be inclined to resist, should it feel a cruel sorrow, and only see the hand of the creature in these trials, do not permit it, Lord, but make me raise my eyes above the earth so as to see only you in all things!

Even should it happen that I fear the Cross, should I at times be tempted to refuse to carry it on my shoulders, should I wish to shun it, never forsake me, my good Jesus. During those stormy days and desolate nights in the midst of the tempest of my life and my fight with temptations, make me always listen to your voice saying to my inmost soul: «Fear not . . . I am your Jesus who visits you, tries you, and loves you». «It is the Lord!»

O Mary, who during your life made it your goal and aim to see Jesus and imitate him in everything, obtain for me the grace always to see him with the eyes of my soul, always to walk in his footsteps and follow him to the summit of Calvary.

Amen.

59. «I AM NOT WORTHY»

My Jesus, I am not worthy to look at you, to stand in your presence, to dwell in this holy house, to live with you under the same roof, breathing the air that you breathe.

O how happy I am in my state of nothingness, and how I wish that this thought of my insignificance would never leave me for a moment! I nurse this thought in my heart, always fearing that it may be taken away from me.

My God, leave it with me. Unite it to me so closely that it may become an integral part of my being.

In the midst of the sorrowful struggles of my life, the knowledge of my great infirmities has been a source of consolation and comfort. I have at least regained my strength in breathing the sweet atmosphere of truth. This delightful rest is a real oasis for my heart. O blessed knowledge of the truth about myself . . . do not leave me . . . be my light, my staff and my support, amidst the storms of pride that sweep over me.

Being what I am, O my God, why would I seek human affection? Why wish to possess what I do not deserve?

Withdraw into your nothingness like a small cloud of smoke which will soon disappear. Hide yourself and annihilate yourself, handful of ashes which the wind will scatter. Your place is on the dunghill, and it is only as a great favor that men endure your presence. You are demented, poor wretch, if you think yourself capable of doing anything but offending God and damning yourself, unless you God comes to your aid. Ah yes, my God, these truths are like balm which refresh the wounds of my soul.

I am not worthy, Lord, to work for your glory. I, in one of the houses of the Cross! And why? And why so much consideration for me?

But who am I, receiving Jesus in a dwelling so unworthy of him!

O Lord, Lord of my Life! Conceal me, hide me, thrust me into the mire, for even a dunghill is too good a throne for me. Nothing is too low for him who has so deeply offended God.

A leper, a cesspool, are both cleaner than I am. Lord! I am nothing but filth and contagion, and yet I want to be esteemed and loved. O Jesus, O Sacred Host, Purity itself! It is into this sink of iniquity that my heart would receive you! Assuage my suffering, my generous Master, as you see how my heart struggles between my unworthiness and my love!

I console myself with the thought that you as the Light of the world cannot suffer or be soiled by contact with me. On the contrary, you cleanse me, and I need to be cleansed and purified to be like an angel. For such as I am, I am not worthy to receive you.

— O my son, these last words please me. Strive to understand them and to practice them in imitation of Mary, and like her, you will draw Jesus into your heart.

Amen.

60. MARTYRDOM

What the martyrs suffered is as nothing, compared to the anguish endured by a soul that possesses God and does not feel his presence.

What torture can be compared with that felt by a soul which is possessed of God and yet apparently abandoned by him! What sufferings these words convey, my Jesus! How bitter the sorrows unknown to the world and only understood by those who love you!

I know by faith that you are with me, but I do not see you. I do not perceive you. I do not touch you. And darkness and temptations, abandonment and all kinds of bitterness paralyze my soul.

My Jesus here present with me within the Sacred Host, this is called the martyrdom of love, more trying and more painful than all the different kinds of martyrdom put together.

O my hidden Lord, how I love you! How you enchant and ravish my soul in spite of your loving disdain!

But why shun me, O my Jesus? What can I say if not that your contempt for me increases my love. The more you avoid me, the more I pursue you, and I know not how to live without Life.

It seems to me that an entire world separates me from you, although, strangely enough, at the same time I feel your heart beating in mine!

It seems to me that a mountain of ice lies between us, although your heart could melt the eternal snows in a moment. A thousand clouds surround me and bar the way and prevent me from approaching that Treasure. A thousand veils envelop me. I cannot tear them asunder in order to contemplate you.

Like a blind man, although I feel your presence in my inmost soul, yet I have no eyes to look at you.

I seem to feel your approach, but my hands are powerless to grasp and hold you.

Your Divine breath is upon me and I remain motionless, ardently longing for the Treasure I have apparently lost, for the Light which seems to be extinguished. I weep and groan and sigh and lament in vain. O my Jesus, where are you, that I do not see you, that I do not perceive you, and that I cannot feel you in my soul, or rather I should say, what is the meaning of this mystery that I see you, that I perceive you, and yet that I do not encounter you!

The days pass, the nights return, the dawn reappears, and in my soul it is all darkness, darkness that can be felt as an intensely cold and bitter suffering.

O Jesus, my heaven, when will daylight come to me!

Have you known the martyrdom, my beloved Mother, of possessing God and not feeling his presence? Ah yes, I do not doubt it for a moment since you are the Queen of Martyrs and you have suffered all that can be suffered. Help me to bear this heavy Cross with love and patience!

Amen.

61. ANGEL, APOSTLE AND MARTYR

I ought to be all three if I am a Christian and if I love Jesus: an angel in purity, an apostle by my prayers, a martyr by my sacrifices! What noble titles are these to which are attached such noble virtues. And if I practice these virtues, they will give me the right to occupy this privileged place where I come to adore you, my Jesus.

But what is it to be an angel?—It is to be pure in thought, word and deed. It is to have a heart transparent as crystal in order to see God, to foresee his wishes, to live in the sunshine of his face, and to understand it. To be an angel is to keep one's wings outstretched ready to fly to do good, to uplift souls to God and to open the gates of heaven for them! To be an angel is to do one's duty and to intercede with God for poor sinners, to see God always and in everything, and never to lose for a single instant the sense of the Divine presence.

To be an angel is to resemble Mary in her immaculate whiteness, in the purity of her thoughts, in the candor of her soul, in the reflection of the Divinity which possessed her, in the innocence of her life, in the simplicity and purity of her heart. O my Jesus, my Light and my Heaven! Give me that purity, for I wish to become an angel to please you!

I must also be an apostle by keeping silence when others talk scandal in my presence, by my speech in defending the honor of my neighbors, in excusing their weaknesses and defects, in speaking of God, of his love, of his goodness and of his charity to all men.

I must be an apostle against too much concern with what others think, in being the first to overcome it. I must be an apostle by my example and above all by my prayers, for it is in praying that my love for my neighbor will increase. Day and night will I beg the graces of heaven for him.

But prayer without sacrifice does not appeal to heaven. In order to be effective, prayer must spring from a mortified heart which has passed through the crucible of suffering, by self-denial, by the Cross.

Angel, apostle, martyr! What a noble mission, my beloved Jesus! But of these three titles, the best known, the one which we can most easily obtain, and which we cannot dispense with, is that of martyr, for who is without a cross in his life? Who passes through this exile without treading upon thorns, without his heart being lacerated and torn asunder? But love makes the cross sweet and pleasant and light. At first the cross is carried with repugnance, then with facility, and finally with love.

It is certain that in the way of the cross it is the first step which counts, for the cross carries him who carries it with love.

The most insignificant cross is precious for the soul, for it establishes the closest union with God. Who can understand this? Only he who has tasted the honey which it encloses, the virtue which is contains, and the peace which it procures.

Dearest Lord, crucify me and give me your love, for with love the soul dares all things, passes through all things, and never tires, for the repose of the soul consists in not reposing.

Martyr, apostle and angel! Obtain for me, O Mary, to be all three in perfection, so as to receive in exchange a triple crown of glory!

Amen.

62. «HE LOVED ME AND DELIVERED HIMSELF FOR ME»

It is in this way that Jesus loves, for he who delivers himself shows the proof of real love. And to what did you deliver yourself, my Jesus? To all kinds of insults, humiliations, poverty, hard work and inconceivable sufferings. But what did all that matter to Jesus, since he loved me?

And I? How do I love you, O my beloved Lord? Can I perhaps say like you I loved him and delivered myself for him? Ah, yes, my Jesus, permit me to tell you that it is true, and that although imperfectly, owing to my great weaknesses, yet I have come here because I loved you, and for this, for this alone, I delivered my body and will to obedience and I wished with the assistance of your grace, to consecrate myself to your service, not in part or in a half-hearted way, but entirely, unreservedly, now and forever.

And truly, my Jesus here present, love alone can deprive man of his liberty. Love alone is capable of making me follow you all the way to death and to all kinds of martyrdom!

The love that crucifies itself, that is the true love. It is the love that delivers itself up without limits and without fear of suffering. And thanks be to you, O my good Jesus, this is the love that I feel for you in this holy place. And in this way, with my soul, with my body, and with my heart, I love you unreservedly without thinking of anything else but loving you, for you alone are worthy of all love.

The love that gives itself always goes ahead and never turns back or repents. It is a love that grows constantly in purity, in fervor and in sacrifice.

Does my love possess all these qualities?

O my Jesus, how much I have to be ashamed of!

Do I shudder at the sight of the Cross? Does my heart tremble in the presence of suffering?

Yes. I do shudder and tremble at times. But, my Jesus, you must make me, in loving you, love suffering also, and place all my delight in imitating you.

I know that to crucify myself is the happy mission that has fallen to my lot, and therefore martyrdom has no terrors for me. Am I not your victim? Must I not here in this House of the Cross, be a faithful copy of him whose life on earth was all suffering?

It is true that there are hidden sorrows which the world ignores, and although sent by you, and known only to you, they make hearts bleed in silence. But these sorrows, while consuming us, preserve and give life, while taking it away.

But this is the mystery of suffering known only to those who love you and deliver themselves up to you, O beloved Jesus. And I wish that you would grant me today the grace to be altogether yours.

This is my sole and most ardent desire: to love you and to deliver myself up for you, in imitation of Mary.

Amen.

63. MIDNIGHT

It seems like a dream that at this solemn hour I should be prostrated at your feet, O my Jesus! At midnight before your resplendent gaze, in this little chapel which has been made for you, in the most perfect solitude, in the most perfect silence which nothing can disturb. Is it possible, O my Jesus? Is it you, Lord, or am I dreaming? Is it I who am thus prostrated at your feet in adoration?

Ah yes, yes, it is you, my Jesus, my only good, my love and my all! It is you who, hidden in this consecrated Host, is gazing at me with a glance of inconceivable tenderness, with a glance whose fire softens the most stubborn hearts, with glances which penetrate into the inmost soul, awaken us to repentance and obtain our pardon.

It is he, my Jesus, who did not want to leave me fatherless, and who found consolation in his Calvary with the thought of making me happy by his continued presence day and night at the altar!

You are he who wished that your Body, and your Blood which was shed, should be my consolation and my joy. And it is so, my beloved Lord, for there is no greater happiness for me on earth than to receive you in Holy Communion, to press you to my heart, to feed on you, to call you mine, to look at you and contemplate you in the Sacred Host without ever being satiated.

It is you, my King, my Master, my Heaven, my All. It is you who are here present, and it is I, wretched and vile creature, who am I here before you. O Lord, look at my tears of gratitude, but do not stop them. Let them moisten these sacred stones, the silent witnesses of my love.

See, Lord, nothing disturbs the majestic silence of the night except this clock which reminds me that the hour of my death is ever coming nearer, that I must become a saint, and love you unto martyrdom. The clock tells me that I have a few minutes less to live, but it is mistaken, for here at your feet, I drink in that life, the life of purity, of self denial, and of love immeasurable. It does not know that I shall not die, because I receive in my heart him who is Life itself. And if I die, what is death but the door which leads me into your arms? But my hour is past, my beloved Lord, and I must tear myself away from your Throne.

O Mary, how much I envy you! Jesus never left you while on earth, and your eyes ever rejoiced in his holy presence. Obtain for me always to see within myself, by the eyes of faith, the Divine presence of the Word made flesh!

Amen.

64. «IF YOU DID KNOW THE GIFT OF GOD»

How tender, how delicate, how sweet are these words which reveal a world of mysteries and the unfathomable depth of tenderness of the Heart of Jesus!

If I knew the gift of God I would undoubtedly be a saint. But what is lacking in me in order to know this gift, to appreciate it, to show my gratitude for it? The spirit of prayer and meditation and the appreciation of the silence of a pure conscience, of the bounty which I have received without deserving it.

The more a man leaves himself, the more room he leaves for God to take possession of him, and to take possession of him is to make him know the gift of God. To reflect on and understand the things of God purifies the soul. To love them makes it Divine. But how can we love them, living as we do in dissipation, shunning every form of holy and pious mediation? O my Eucharistic Jesus, teach me to pray. Teach me that kind of prayer and meditation which leaves the soul luminous and transparent as crystal!

Give me also that spirit of prayer which touches your Heart, my Jesus, that prayer apparently silent, but which fills the heavens with joy in the fullness of its gratitude for all your bounties.

«Why do you shout at me» God said to Moses, who had scarcely opened his lips. For that fervent, steadfast prayer from the bottom of his heart, sounded like thunder in the ears of God. It is that kind of prayer that I desire, which finds an echo in your heart and reechoes in my poor soul, making it know the gift of God.

Do not grieve, my beloved Master. With the aid of your grace I shall yet know this gift which will make me happy and will give me heaven.

Forgive me if up to now I have made such poor use of your graces and favors. I promise to dedicate myself from now on with fervor to prayer and meditation. And if I can do nothing else, I shall at least rejoice in suffering for your honor.

O Mary, you who more than any other creature received the gift of God, obtain for us your children to receive it likewise and to appreciate and profit by it!

Amen.

65. ABUSE OF GRACES

This is my crime, O my God, the abuse of your graces, and I tremble at the thought.

I have spent so many years in your service, O my Beloved Jesus! I have made so many confessions and received so many Communions, and have been overwhelmed with such a torrent of graces! Am I more humble? More mortified? More detached from the world and from myself?

How many are there on earth who would have become saints with the least of the graces I have received. And I, wretched sinner, have rejected and spurned them!

Have I even appreciated the value of grace which has been purchased at the price of the blood of Jesus?

I call to mind the barren fig tree in the Gospel, and the thought occurs to me that, after all, I may be living in this house of God to no purpose, that I may be a barren tree without fruit for life eternal.

«Cut it down, why encumber the ground?» said the Lord to the gardener. And I, am I certain that I am not running the same risk if I continue to lead this idle and aimless life with the same routine, with no energy to conquer myself, taking so little account of my innumerable failings?

In deceiving others, one ends up deceiving oneself. Could this not be the case with me?

O my God how great are my sins and how malicious my faults! Who could count them?

How many sins forgotten, how many more committed thoughtlessly, and how many of which I am not even conscious!

How much culpable ignorance, deliberate inadvertence, voluntary rebellion, vain fantasies, uncharitable words, innumerable omissions, and, above all, what negligence in failing to profit by the graces received!

On a thousand occasions I have felt within me Divine inspirations and have blamably rejected them.

How often has the Lord offered me graces of self-denial, humility and sacrifice, and I, wretch that I am, have not made the least effort to profit by them.

O my Jesus, hidden here within the Sacred Host! What can I say but to ask you in your goodness to pardon me, to have patience with me, and to wait for me to correct my faults!

Today, this very moment, I will begin a life of love that will correspond with your grace. I promise you, my Jesus, but O!, help me, have pity on me, for my weakness is great!

O Mary, nobody was ever more faithful than you to the interior voice of the Holy Spirit. Obtain for me the grace to correspond faithfully to the inspirations of grace!

Amen.

66. IT IS BUT JUSTICE

Yes, Lord, it is just that I should suffer, that I should bear the weight of my suffering, for I have sinned and offended you, O my beloved Jesus! If you, my Love, who clothed yourself in sin in order to expiate it, said that it was just that you should be plunged in the ocean of sorrow and humiliation which filled your life, what shall I say who am sin itself? Is it not just that I should suffer and live a life of immolation in sacrificing myself and in letting myself be sacrificed in honor of you? If you always chose suffering, dare I seek anything else?

— Yes, my dear son, it is true that I, during my sojourn on earth and solely because I loved you, always chose what was most painful and humiliating, most shameful and cruel. And you must live my life of victim and abandon yourself to my will.

Abandon yourself unreservedly, and in everything that my will presents to you. Seek always what is most painful, what will cost you most and rend your heart the most. What will humiliate you most and make your soul bleed most abundantly. For it is just that you should suffer for the sins of others as well as for your own.

In your everyday life, profit by and even look for opportunities of humiliating yourself and of suffering, without ever being discouraged by your infidelities or weaknesses. Every day, my son, you will discover new fields to conquer if you reduce your will to nothing, if you give up your own judgment and lacerate your heart in seeking the cross of suffering for love of me and rejoicing when you have found it.

— O my Jesus here present with me, how beautiful are the lessons you have wished to teach me today. I will take them to heart and in practicing them I will attach myself with you to the Cross.

From now on I will joyfully accept all that you ask. I wish to live that life of suffering, the life which transforms and sanctifies. Do you hear me, my Jesus?

— Yes, I hear my beloved one. Suffer and fear not. Open your wings, fly to the sacrifice of yourself, and love me as I love you, as I have always loved you. For you must love me with the same love.

At every humiliation, at every trial, whether from God or man, at every trouble and at every sorrow, repeat, my son, as you think deeply of their meaning, these words which will fortify while humbling you: It is just that I, a sinner, should suffer in union with Innocence itself, with him who is Love.

— Yes, my Jesus, this is what I desire to do in order to imitate more perfectly your Mother and mine, who, although innocent, wished to unite her sufferings to yours in order to appease the justice of the Eternal Father.

Amen.

67. IMMOLATION

What is it that cost me most today? Is it to conquer myself, to humble myself, to lay bare my heart, to crush my pride, to go in search of suffering, of the Cross which I have avoided up till now through cowardice and lack of generosity?

I know well enough what it is that costs me the most today, and what has kept me back on the way to perfection, what my conscience reproaches me for every time that I examine myself, and what fills me with remorse when I least expect it.

Prostrate at your feet during the time of my adoration, O my Jesus here present, when your Divine light illuminates my soul, when I see you stretching out your arms to me, asking me for what I have refused you so long, how can I possibly not respond to all the tender proofs of your affection? Here at your feet once more will I have the courage to say «No» to you, so as not to hurt my pride, nor lose the esteem of my neighbors, nor break off a friendship, nor lacerate my heart, even when I see you bleeding and pierced with thorns?

O, no, my Jesus, my Life, I cannot resist your appeal. I can no longer refuse to renounce myself and to say «No» in place of «Yes», and «Yes» instead of «No». I must give up my own will in order to do yours and to love you more.

What does it matter if from now on I humiliate myself, if in so doing I please you?

Sacrifice all that I am and all that I have, honor, friendships, admiration, soul and life itself?

O my beloved Jesus, your glances captivate my heart. Your patience in waiting for me makes me blush. Your tenderness overcomes me. Your goodness overwhelms me.

I will sacrifice myself for you. I know what costs me the most and with the help of Mary, my most loving Mother, I will joyfully sacrifice it to you on the altar of my heart.

Give your poor child courage, my Jesus, and urge him to crucify himself for love of you!

Amen.

68. THE CRY OF THE SOUL

My Life! My Jesus! My Heaven! My Delight! My Joy! My Happiness! My God!

O my Jesus here present with me, my adored Word, my Good, my Treasure! What can I say to you when there exist no words and phrases to interpret the feelings of my soul or which my heart, burning for love of you, could communicate to you?

All earthly loves combined are as nothing compared to the love which consumes my heart. are but empty gestures, compared to those inner feelings which absorb me, transport me, rip me out of myself and make me tremble and die of love.

The softest sounds seem painful, gentleness is harsh, melody is without attraction, all sweetness is bitter, light is darkness when I think of your indescribable love in the Eucharist, that predilection for your child, vile earthworm that I am, which gives rise in me to a thousand feelings of angelic, heavenly and Divine love.

O Jesus who gives me life! O my Lord, who does not disdain to take up your dwelling in this most worthless heart. What shall I say to you but what I have already said? You have come to unite yourself to the vilest dross. Your humility obliges me to humble myself, and the part of Victim that you have chosen impels me to sacrifice myself.

I feel that I must live only for this, to suffer and to humble myself continually.

My soul must nevermore be separated from this consecrated Host, and my body will be the wood, the fire, the incense which are consumed in honor of you.

Grant me, my good Jesus, Love of my loves, the grace to be ever faithful to the Divine inspiration which impels me to detest myself, to humiliate myself, to crucify myself in the silence of an interior life, all purity, oblivion and sacrifice!

Mary, Mother of my soul, obtain for me from your Jesus this joy of yours, you who are of all creatures and has always been the purest, the most hidden, the most crucified.

Amen.

69. WHAT FOR?

O my Jesus, living as I do in this holy house in the warmth of your care and your love, why do I still seek what the least gust of wind scatters while rending the heart: human affection, admiration, approbation, tenderness?

Why am I so given to attaching myself to what passes and vanishes leaving an emptiness around me?

Why do I seek human praise, and interest myself in those frivolous trifles which diminish your presence in my soul?

Why do I waste time in vain arguments, in self-love, in building castles in the air, in thoughts which torture the heart in vain?

Why do I seek peace, joy and happiness outside the Cross in all its forms?

Why take trouble to escape the trials to which the Lord wishes to subject my body and soul?

Why desire anything else than to humiliate and sacrifice myself every day more and more?

Why do I wander seeking repose for my soul, when I know well enough that it is only to be found at the foot of the Cross?

Why do I desire ardently anything else except to be crucified by God and man?

Why tire myself in vain endeavors to find out how to belong more to you, when I know that I shall only reach this goal by renouncing myself unceasingly for love of you?

Why seek for joy elsewhere than in mortification and in complete immolation of my whole being on the altar of the purest, most disinterested and most generous love?

Why, alas, do I say that I love God so much, when I love not mortification?

Why do I seek for you and not for suffering which possesses the virtue to purify and the grace to unite the soul to its Beloved?

Why waste my time with theories about virtues and not apply myself fervently to tear myself out of myself and from all I love, making out of my heart a living lamp which consumes itself for you, my beloved Jesus?

Why desire treasures other than humiliations, and to be treated with contempt by my neighbors as the scum of the earth? Do I not know that I must disappear from the heart of man, and that I must strive to be the least of all in the eyes of men, and secretly the greatest of all in the eyes of God?

O my Jesus, my Jesus, my place is in heaven and not on earth . . . in that Divine Heart, in that consecrated Host. Grant me, then, the grace to live and die consumed in this furnace of love!

Amen.

70. HEAR ME

Hear me, O Lord, and grant me what I come to ask of you today.

The most fervent desire of my heart is that I may accomplish your divine will and respond to your designs for my poor soul. Make them known to me, my Jesus, so that my life may be a continuous and unceasing act of love.

Make me understand that all actions which do not honor you by their purity of intention, are valueless.

Make me understand that all my acts of piety should not be done out of mere routine, but that they should be, as it were, an urgent necessity of love for my heart.

O my Jesus here present with me, my Joy and my Life! Grant me the grace to be humble and not to seek myself, not to lose sight of you during my conversations, nor to be cast down in my sorrow, nor to appear restrained in my devotions, but to be austere without showing it, always keeping a smile on my lips.

Teach me also to speak straightforwardly, to fear the Lord without being despondent, to hope without presumption, to allow myself to be criticized without losing my peace of mind, to love my neighbors sincerely, to edify them without seeking to attract attention, to obey without a murmur, and to suffer without complaint.

O Jesus, fountain of all good, give me a heart full of love for you, which nothing can divert from you, a faithful and generous heart which never hesitates nor stumbles in the way of the Cross; an invincible heart, ever disposed to renew the struggle after each skirmish; a heart free from all attachment and enslaved by no passions . . . an upright heart which never seeks a devious path.

Give me a mind, Lord, incapable of misunderstanding you, and one that is constantly seeking you.

Lord, may my soul await the manifestation of your will and trust in your Divine word, always full of faith and confidence.

My Jesus, be my light in darkness and my consolation in trials.

Let me find my happiness in pleasing you and let me seek your adorable will and find and do it all the days of my life.

Have you heard me, my Jesus? O yes, always hear the cry of the loving soul which only aspires to forget itself in order to find you alone.

Grant me today, my good Lord, all these favors through the intercession of my Mother and yours!

Amen.

71. TO ESTIMATE THINGS AT THEIR TRUE VALUE

My Jesus, this is what I need within me. The day when I succeed in estimating things at their true value, my soul will cease to be disturbed by manifestations of self-love and the foolish resentments of my heart will subside.

After so many years I still have not thoroughly appreciated what I am and what I deserve.

I have not pondered sufficiently the reason for my entrance into this religious community.

I have not thoroughly appreciated the fact that it is the Lord who has granted me the favor of calling me into his service, rather than I who have granted a favor to him in coming here to subject myself to the virtues of obedience, poverty and chastity.

I have not appreciated until now the unique grace of my vocation to the Cross, nor the significance of the celestial mission which is implied in this vocation. I have not properly understood the fact that I became a Religious in order to serve and not to be served. And I have not thoroughly understood that I have come here to renounce my own will and judgment, and to do the will of my superiors, which is the will of God for me.

I came here to be as a little child with all a child's qualities, to cease to be what I was in order to acquire the special virtues of the little ones: simplicity, candor, innocence, entire renunciation of my will, with an absolute confidence in the commands of my superiors.

A little child does not criticize or find fault or judge. He lets himself be led right and left, up and down, without troubling about the future, because it is not his. He always believes what he is told, and in the presence of danger it is sufficient for him to throw himself with unlimited trust into the arms of his mother as he thoroughly believes all she tells him.

O my Jesus here present! Give me today the docility of little children so that I may draw nearer to you. Make me fully understand that this community is a mother to me, and that I am its little child who must nourish myself on the holy teachings to be found in its bosom, in the fruitful shadow of the Cross. Make me become a child so that I may enter into the Kingdom of Heaven.

Lord, let me open my eyes on the light of this altar, at the sight of this beloved Monstrance, in order to thoroughly appreciate my utter insignificance and to understand that I have not merited the very slightest favor from your hands.

Let me thoroughly understand that death awaits me at no distant date, and that I must use the few remaining days of my life in sacrificing myself and loving him who is love itself, in union with Mary.

Amen.

72. MY SORROWS ARE NOT SORROWS . . .

O, my beloved Jesus, however much I suffer, however bitter is the pain, my sorrows are not sorrows, but your sorrows are my sorrows. Every form of bitter suffering disappears in the face of your sufferings in the garden of Olives, and all my tortures vanish when I gaze upon the Cross!

I lose sight of my torments when I contemplate yours. And, then, in however great tribulation is my soul, I say to myself, my sorrows are not sorrows, his sorrows are my sorrows!

The more I suffer humiliation, the more I feel that my humiliations are as nothing compared to those that filled your heart.

Can my sufferings of poverty and want, of hunger and thirst ever equal yours?

How can I ever compare the sufferings which may fall to my lot with those you have undergone in your apostolic labors?

In contemplating your perpetual sacrifice, your desolation and most cruel abandonment, O my Jesus, what can I say but that all my sufferings are as nothing compared to yours?

You kept for yourself all that was most cruel in your trials. You took all sufferings on yourself. You rendered suffering Divine! As a Lamb, you did not open your mouth when you were led to be crucified. You stretched out your hands to be nailed to the Cross. You went forth to meet humiliation and contempt!

And what shall I say of your interior sorrows, of the agonies of your Heart? What of that thirst for souls which consumed you, of that insatiable hunger for the glory of your heavenly Father which devoured you?

What did you feel then, O my sweetest Jesus, and what do you still feel at the boundless ingratitude of men and especially of myself?

O folly of the Cross which I love with all my heart! And if my sorrows are worth nothing, make me partake more and more of yours, to suffer at your side for the same cause . . . and to be lacerated with the thorns which lacerated you.

I want to weep when you weep, O my Jesus!

Although I am worth nothing, I want, like you, to become a victim on behalf of sinners.

My sorrows are not sorrows, they are treasures. My humiliations are triumphs, and pearls of great price, for the remembrance of you renders sweet all that is bitter.

O beloved Jesus, what constitutes my sorrow is to see:

souls going to perdition;
you being outrageously offended;
the loss of faith;
your graces perpetually rejected;
sensuality invading all hearts;
the reign of Satan;
the persecution of the Church;
your heavenly Father outraged;
the Cross an object of abhorrence.

Ah yes, my Jesus, these sorrows kill me because they are your sorrows and they wound you to the heart. That is why your sorrows are my sorrows and also why my sorrows are not sorrows at all.

Amen.

73. GOD AND I

O my God, the center of my being and my Life. When will you be the only guest of my heart and my all?

Why do I seek for affection, and friends, and a thousand other things, which are not you? That is why I am troubled, why I suffer, because I divide my heart with creatures, when I should seek you alone, my Creator, my Lord, for you alone can fill the infinite depths of my soul!

Let my poor heart bleed today at Your feet, let me cast away from me love of all creatures . . . all self-love and empty fantasies.

Heal me, O heavenly Physician, cauterize my wounds, and let me no more seek on earth what does not exist, what you do not wish me to find.

You know that I no longer look for the good opinion of my neighbors.

Have I not chosen to live happily in oblivion, forsaken, forgotten and despised by those I love? Have I not asked you a thousand times that I may not occupy a place in the hearts of others, that you alone should occupy them, and that they should forget me forever?

Have I not told you that I wish to suffer alone with you . . . that I will always offer You the first fruits of my sorrows, and keep in the innermost depths of my heart the mystery, the sweet, sweet secret of the Cross.

Have I not promised You that all my mental and physical sufferings shall be for You alone?

Why then do I seek for consolation, where I cannot find it?

If I lose a worldly affection, does not your heart belong, then, the more to me?

Even if you should deprive me of consolation and plunge me into despair, is not the Holy Spirit my Divine Comforter?

If I am on the point of falling, are you not my strength?

If my heart is full of bitterness, is it not you who has put the chalice to my lips?

How long, Lord, will I delay before I fly to You without waiting to gratify self-love, earthly satisfactions and the relief which sensuality craves: things which wound in a thousand ways and make me lose to a great extent the merit of my sufferings?

O my Lord, Master of my life, when will the day arrive when my consolation shall be to have no consolation for love of you?

Grant, me, O Jesus here present with me, the grace to suffer in union with you without imperfection. Make me seek you, and, only after having found you, seek those whom you have given as guides to lead me to your Heart.

O Mary, obtain for us in our sorrows to seek, like you, no consolation except in the Heart of Jesus!

Amen.

74. IT IS SWEET TO SUFFER

Yes, my beloved Jesus, it is very sweet for the loving heart to suffer, and it seems to live but lifelessly when it is deprived of the Cross.

To live on the Cross is to live on love, and who would live without love?

«Ask, said St. Augustine, the gift of prophecy, ask for wisdom, humility, patience, chastity; as for me, I ask only for charity, which is the greatest of all virtues, and all others are subordinate to it».

Even if God should give me all He possesses, if He denies me charity, He denies me himself. But love takes fire, keeps itself lit and increases by suffering; voluntary suffering is its only fuel.

«The Cross has wings, said St. Augustine, and they help to lift us out of this valley of tears, to raise us to the serene region of heaven».

It is only on the heights of Calvary life is found, perfect peace and pure happiness.

Subjection to the Cross frees the soul from slavery and gives strength and true happiness.

Under these circumstances, then, is not suffering to be envied?

Yes, a thousand times, since You my Lord, constituted yourself a victim, and in traveling through boundless space quit heaven to live as a martyr and to die on the Cross. You deprived suffering of its bitterness: after being nailed to the Cross, you poured honey on the bitterness of life. Is not suffering, then, to be envied?

When the soul, crushed like a grape, is oppressed with the weight of the Cross, it produces a liquor which nourishes and fortifies.

Since You, Lord, by your contact have rendered suffering Divine, the thorns produce the sweetest balm, and the Cross delicious fruits, but in order that the thorns and the Cross should give forth their treasures, it is necessary to press the former in one's hands and the latter in one's heart.

That is what I wish, O my Jesus, to produce that balm to heal your wounds and to give you consolation: let me be pierced with the thorns and nailed to the Cross, for all this is so sweet for the heart which loves you.

The outside of the Cross appears dry and hard and rugged, but if one penetrates to the heart of the Cross, the most delicious oil and the most exquisite honey are there to be found. For it is there that the soul meets you, my Jesus, my Beloved, and, at your side and in union with you, can there be anything but heaven?

Let suffering come, then, my Jesus, for only in suffering does my soul find repose.

O Mary, Queen of Sorrows, help me to love and suffer like Jesus and like you!

Amen.

75. LOVE, CONSOLATION

To love you, Jesus and to console you! These words make up my life.

O Jesus, love is the source of all my encounters with you. Your consolation is the object of all my efforts. But between these two points what a wide field of suffering! What chasms to be traversed with a thousand ways of suffering! What struggles to be undergone. What bleeding of the heart. What torments and what martyrdom! Yet my heart does not fear suffering and is not upset by it.

All tortures are as nothing to me provided that in suffering them I do so in order to glorify you, to console you, to please you, and to make you rejoice.

O Jesus, my tears are of no account, provided that they prevent you from shedding yours.

My wounds do not, and will not, count if through them yours may be healed.

My sorrows are nothing if they alleviate yours.

What does it matter if my heart is sorely wounded and lacerated with thorns if by this means I can tear out the thorns which lacerate yours?

Let ingratitude break my heart provided that you no longer feel the ingratitude of the world which can burst the delicate fibers of your heart.

Ah, my Jesus! What an immense joy to live in suffering in order to console you.

Happy would he be who could take on himself all the ingratitude of men, the contempt, the insults, the hatred, the blasphemies, the innumerable sins that have been committed, in order to expiate them so that you, my Jesus, would not have to suffer for them anymore.

My Jesus, without you we are nothing, and without your Divine merits none of our actions can be a source of merit or of expiation.

Come, then, my Jesus, my Heaven, my Beloved! Come to help me and give some value to my love! Give to me in order that I may give to you who are all powerful! I ask you for consolations to console you, for remedies to alleviate your sufferings, for an intense and immense love of sacrifice to love you.

For what can love not do? It can undertake all things, conquer all difficulties and remove all obstacles!

Of all strong things, love is the strongest. Let it come then to sacrifice me, to devour me, to absorb me, to consume me in the Heart of my Beloved!

Love and consolation! You have always found them in the heart of Mary. Grant that in every heart which beats in unison with yours in the Houses of the Cross, you will also find Love and consolation!

Amen.

76. AT NIGHTFALL

The sun has gone down and the light has disappeared . . . but I do not fear because I am near to a Sun that never sets . . . to a Light of Lights which is never hidden. I am at the foot of the Tabernacle, bathed in the supernatural light of the Sacred Host. What does it matter to me that the world is enveloped in darkness? It does not affect me . . . Reposing in the Heart of Jesus, I fear nothing. Jesus whispers to me in this loved solitude that if I love him, he will be my heaven on earth, my consolation in my exile, my light, which can never be extinguished, the mysterious fire which envelops me with its Divine heat.

Ah yes! I love him with a unique love, with a love most detached and most pure, with an incomparable love, unsurpassable, indestructible and insatiable; with a love as vast as the immensity of my soul!

I love him with a love marked with the seal of blood through suffering and voluntary crucifixion. I love him ardently, with a love with which God alone can be loved. That is why I do not fear the darkness of night. That is why my heart is full of light, for Jesus is there in all his eternal splendor, for the effect of his Divine presence in Holy Communion makes itself felt still in my heart. For with him it is always dawn in my soul, it is always day, and the shades of night always shun his brightness.

The hour of twilight has something solemn about it, as I abide at the foot of the Tabernacle in the warmth and shelter of the Host. It seems like the hour of a meeting of lovers when Jesus waits for the soul which flies to his breast, he who will load it with graces. Exhausted with the burden and heat of the day, the soul comes like a dove to repose on the Divine breast of Jesus, in the arms of the Beloved, and then, «far from the madding crowd», they communicate to each other their most secret thoughts and confidences, drawing together more and more the bonds of love which unite them.

Heavenly moments are those which are passed after «the knell of parting day», at the foot of the Tabernacle! How full of charm is that hour for a soul which only lives on thoughts of heaven! O my hidden Jesus! Will that be the hour, the happy hour, when I will burst asunder the bonds that bind me to earth, and enter into the immensity of the love of God? I am going, my Jesus, but not into the darkness of night, for I carry with me the light which is never extinguished.

O Mary, when my last evening on earth will arrive, fly to me, my beloved Mother, and help me to pass through the darkness of this life into the eternal light.

Amen.

77. MARY IS THE STEM, JESUS THE FLOWER

Mary is the tree, Jesus is the sweetest of fruits, fed to us in Holy Communion. Mary is the stem, Jesus the Flower. But why is Mary so precious a tree as to have gained for us the Flower of flowers, the Fruit of fruits? It is because she was a living cross, which is bound to produce a Divine flower, a Lily bathed in blood, an Immaculate Jesus.

The Cross is the mother of purity. Therefore, how could Mary, the Queen of Sorrows, the Empress of Martyrs, produce anything else?

O Mary most pure, most holy, without the semblance of a stain, make me pure and fervent. Obtain for me that celestial fire which I need in order to love him who is Love itself.

I have come to this holy dwelling attracted by its heavenly perfumes. O Mystical Rose, obtain for me grace to inhale them, that I may be steeped in the aroma of the celestial virtues which emanate from the Holy Eucharist.

With your substance you have fed that same Jesus who every day gives me life, your life, O Mary, that very life which he owes you.

Every drop of his blood you gave him so that it should be mine.

With your virgin milk you fed him so that he might die on the Cross and open the gates of heaven for me.

My beloved Mother, it is to you, then, that I owe the happiness which I enjoy in contemplating him.

He derived the light from your eyes, the color from your cheeks, the flesh from your flesh, and a heart from your heart, to be pierced by my ingratitude. Yes, O my Mother, you gave me Jesus, the Word made Flesh, who at this moment I am contemplating in the Host.

In his glory, he had no tears to shed. He came, alas, to take them from your eyes. He had no blood to redeem me, but in making himself man he came to take it from your veins. He had no body to be cruelly scourged and beaten and nailed on the Cross. He waited for you to pronounce the words: «Behold the slave of the Lord», in order to take his immaculate Body from you!

O Mary, without you there would be neither Holy Eucharist, nor Tabernacle. There would be no Jesus, the blessed fruit of your womb, for me to adore and imitate in crucifying myself.

How can I ever show you my gratitude, my Mother? O blessed Virgin, I can only do so by imitating your hidden virtues: the purity of your soul imitated by purifying mine in repentance and penitence. I want to be pure as you are and a victim as he was. I want to give him all my love and take refuge in his sorrows!

Obtain for me the grace never to be separated from the Cross, always to be identified with it. Wretched and miserable as I am, I want to take up this fruit, this Jesus, in my arms, this heart of fire which consumes and embraces me, which does not let me fall, which pierces me with its thorns and envelops me with its celestial light.

O my Mother, let me gather from its stalk the Lily of the Valleys! Let me pluck from this tree the Delicious Fruit which you carry in your arms. I want to breathe it, inhale it, feed on it, press it to the icy coldness of my heart and sacrifice myself for him in always loving him more and more!

Amen.

78. «I HAVE GIVEN YOU AN EXAMPLE FOR YOU TO DO AS I HAVE DONE»

What were the actions of Jesus? How were the hours and minutes of his most holy life spent? An uninterrupted chain of acts of heroic virtues and an uninterrupted act of love and sacrifice.

Love and sacrifice, such as the life of our sweetest Savior. From the Manger to the Cross, from his incarnation to his death, Jesus did not pass a day or an hour, not a single instant, without humiliations and crosses.

In those two virtues of humility and sacrifice the fiery ardor of his love seemed to increase always more and more. Life of my life, my most loving Jesus! Love was your executioner, that love which impelled you to embrace the folly of the Cross! I wish it to be mine. To be humiliated and to suffer, to be humiliated beyond measure and to immolate myself unceasingly!

O Jesus, give me that thirst for humiliation which you always had, that eagerness for suffering which you were never able to satisfy completely! O my Jesus, have I not cause to be ashamed, I, who am so proud and so slothful in good works!

O Life of my soul, O God of love! Transform my heart into yours so that I may know how to suffer and to love humiliations and crosses. O Lord, you provided me with examples during your short life, and you gave me your blood, your strength and your honor. To be my model, you practiced all the most perfect virtues. In order to save me, you gained infinite merits for my salvation.

O my Jesus, you desire me to imitate you, to act like you. I am utterly confused when I consider the contrast between my so sinful life and your so innocent life, between my sensuality and the austerity with which you treated your most holy Body. Lord, you did not break a reed. You did not put out the still smoking fuse. How great is the merciful tenderness of your heart! Your words were as milk and honey. You called yourself the Son of man! What humility! You said: «Let the little children come unto me». What kindness! You passed through the world doing good. You saved the woman taken in adultery. When you were yourself parched with thirst you gave mysterious water to the Samaritan woman! What thoughtfulness, what goodness, what charity!

In exchange for a glass of cold water, you promised an eternal reward. What gratitude! You forgive and forget, O Lord. St. Peter and St. Mary Magdalene can bear witness to it. You put our sins on your shoulders that you may see them no more. You efface them with your blood and cast them into the sea that they may pass out of your sight.

«Come to me all you that labor and are burdened and I will give you rest. Ask and you shall receive. Knock and it shall be opened unto you.» All these are your words: they breathe nothing but goodness and love.

And what poverty! You had not even a stone on which to lay your head! And what obedience! Obedient unto death, even unto death on the Cross! And what gentleness! Learn from me for I am meek. What goodness! It was said of you: Goodness has appeared in the world. What abnegation! You gave your life not only for your friends, but for your enemies as well. And what a Heart! Even after death it was opened to give me life!

O Jesus, O love of God! O God of love! Take from me all that is not yourself. Make me ashamed of the life I have led up till now. I will try to imitate you, my Jesus, but you who are my hope, help me, for without you I must remain what I am.

O Mary, who must have heard the Divine words «I have given you an example for you to do as I have done», you always imitated Jesus by copying him in your most loving heart. Make us, your children, also do as Jesus did, so that we may carry our cross to be crucified on it, in honor and in love of the beloved Father!

Amen.

79. HERE AM I

Yes, my Jesus, here I am. It is my earnest wish during the hour that I am going to spend at your feet to multiply my demands, my desires, and my acts of love.

What do I ask of you, O my sweetest Jesus? I ask you for a heart like yours. I ask for your own Heart. I ask you, O Jesus, spouse of my soul, to possess only you. Lord, many things disturb me, trouble me, distract me, hurt me, because they separate me from you.

O my Jesus, I am very poor. I come to your altar to receive light, to know myself and to despise myself, to receive the strength to conquer my passions, to beat down my pride, to crucify my flesh and my affections, to sacrifice my will and my opinions; to kill that self by means of the Cross, to humiliate myself so that you may reign, and to disappear so that others may appear.

I want also to multiply my desires because there is a martyrdom of desire with which you are well pleased.

My Jesus, I desire to see you known and imitated . . . I desire to suffer much for you who has suffered so much for me. I desire to give you millions of souls, cost what they may, and to buy them with the price of suffering.

I ask you to give me a pure soul, transparent as crystal, in which your Divinity and your holy Humanity are reflected. I want them to be imprinted on it with ineffaceable marks. O that I were another Jesus crucified, with his patience, his gentleness and his charity for others!

I desire to be enriched by you, that in my turn I may enrich others. I desire to receive light from you, grace, life, fervor, love, so that I may communicate them to others.

I desire to shed my blood. I desire martyrdom, the cross, millions of crosses, in order to be nailed to them for love of you.

I desire your glory, your greatest glory, even if in order to obtain it I would be obliged to walk barefoot on a thousand thorns.

I desire most ardently the salvation of souls and to suffer martyrdom when I realize my powerlessness to snatch them from sin and perdition.

I desire, above all things, to love you immeasurably, and I wish to speak to you now of the love that I wish I could have for you.

O my sweetest fire of love! O life of my soul, and heart of my heart! This is what I want to ask of you: to love you and that you may be my only Love. I am far from loving you as I want to, because I live as it were too close to myself, and at my approach everything is chilled and soiled in contact with me. O my Jesus, even though I am so worthless, I know that you desire my love. Give me, then, that real love which transforms the soul and sanctifies it.

O Jesus, more closely united to me than the most intimate part of my soul, why won't you absorb me, consume me and make me melt in your Divine love?

What stops you from working in me what you desire? Come to me, for without you I am utterly incapable of loving you.

O Mary, obtain for me the ability to love him who is Love itself!

Amen.

80. «I LOVE YOU AS MY FATHER HAS LOVED ME»

O my beloved Jesus, thank you for that special love which crucifies the soul while filling it with heavenly blessings.

— O my son, in order to merit this happiness, you must surrender yourself into the hands of God with love and through love: sweetly, patiently, gently and modestly, and with an all consuming fiery love. You must have a desire to burst through all obstacles, a contempt for all created things, living a life entirely supernatural and Divine.

And if I love you as my Father has loved me, you must love him as I do, with that love which exalts, gives merit to and sanctifies all things.

— O Jesus, my soul's beloved! Love me, then, as your Father loved you, by crucifying me for others! What a blessed mission, to suffer in body and soul for one's friends and one's enemies without their knowledge . . . to crucify oneself, and to live a life of suffering without knowing for what or for whom . . . to purchase graces, Lord, with that unique coin which circulates in heaven, for thousands of souls that I will not know until the Last Day.

But all this must be in union with you, for without you of what avail would be all my sacrifices?

How can I be sure of my way, if I separate myself from you and from your Cross? For the Cross leads to you, Jesus of my soul, and if I follow it, I shall meet you without delay. I know the path I must follow if I should happen to lose you. «The Lord has passed through here», my heart will tell me, and in the end I shall find you.

Make me always follow in your footsteps, and never turn your eyes or your Cross away from me. The Eternal Father acted in this way with you, looking at you and crucifying you. In the same way, with me you must do the same, O Heaven of my life! Look at me with one of those glances which create saints, that through the virtue of this glance I may joyfully let myself be crucified!

I desire to follow you even though I would be lacerated with thorns in doing so. I wish to imitate you. With you I wish to be crucified. Here are my feet, my hands, my body, my heart. Take them, Lord, and accept them for the sake of anyone you may choose.

I renounce all possession of myself. I give over to you my powers, my senses, and my will.

I renounce also, O my soul's Beloved, all the personal benefits I could receive from my prayers, communions, penances, masses, sufferings and sorrows, giving them all through the hands of Mary to your loving Father, even to my last breath, so that he may use whatever may be good in them in any way he thinks best. This is my only desire.

Lord, if you would love me as your most loving Father loved you, in sacrificing you for love, make me also to love him as you loved him, and always to do his will with joy.

Amen.

81. JESUS WILLS IT

And I also! His will is my good and my life. What does it matter that nature protests and wishes to escape from suffering! My soul will triumph through these simple words: «Thy will be done on earth, Lord, as it is in Heaven!»

«Jesus wills it». What beautiful words these are which penetrate to the bottom of my heart and make it leap with joy!

Are they not capable of softening an ocean of bitterness? O my God, who is all goodness and mercy! Will my heart ever be able to resist your desires and your goodness. Ah, no, for I want to please you in executing the very smallest desires of your heart.

O my Jesus, I will say to you with St. Augustine, «Give me what you ask of me, and ask me what you will».

What am I without you? A grain of dust is of more value than this miserable creature who has known how to offend you but has been unable to weep for his sins!

How much time do I spend caring for this wretched body, looking after myself, obeying my caprices, and living without even thinking what you wanted from me. I have spent my life in satisfying and pleasing myself. But now, Jesus, pardon me. I bitterly regret having reigned alone for so long in my heart, and I wish it to be no longer that way.

From now on your will shall be my will, and your pleasure my pleasure.

If it be your will that sorrows should surround me, that bitterness should overwhelm me, that tribulation and crosses should be my lot, I will smilingly say, even with tears: «Jesus wills it, and I also».

If death takes away from me the beings I love best, I will say, in the midst of my deep affliction, «Jesus wills it». He knows why. It is his will and that is enough for me.

When I am bent under the weight of the Cross, when my strength fails me and complaints are on the tip of my tongue, I will force them back and say with resignation, «Jesus wills it and I also».

What does it matter if I succumb and die because of the intensity of my sufferings if Jesus wills it to be that way? He will be with me, near me, even though I will not see him or feel his presence!

He loves me and that is enough for me. He will not allow me to be tempted beyond my strength, and should it be exhausted, he will help me. He is a good Cyrenean who almost makes me wish to fall under the weight of my sufferings that I may see him coming to my assistance!

I know what you wish for me, my Jesus. I know that the cross is my legacy and the thorns my inheritance. O happy lot, enviable destiny which even the angels could court!

Can there exist a greater happiness than to suffer for you, Love of all loves? Ah, no, impossible, for you love those who are crucified, and give them your life. You give them a foretaste of heaven! Lord, I deliver myself up to suffer more and more, and I prefer the Cross with you to all earthly joys without you.

O Mary, Jesus wishes us to carry our crosses after him, in imitation of you, every moment of our lives. Such is our part as victims, in imitation of the two victims of Calvary: Jesus and you. Ah yes, we also wish it, as you well know. O Mother, we have no other will but that of Jesus!

82. DO YOU REMEMBER?

— O my son, my heart's beloved, do you remember the day, the hour, the exact moment in which I whispered to you: «I wish you to be pure, I wish you to be holy, I wish you to be mine»?

You opened to me the flower of your soul, and I, with much love, implanted in it the seed of the vocation to the Cross.

From that moment the seed began to germinate in your heart, making you experience the emptiness of the world, the need for an infinite good, giving you an ardent desire for heaven. Do you remember?

The world and its pleasures, Satan and his creatures plotted against you. The storms that come from unconquered passions made you turn away from your path. But, then, a thousand crosses met you and stopped you on the way: crosses of deception, of disillusionment, crosses of loneliness within your heart, which made you turn your gaze towards me who was awaiting you smiling with open arms. Do you remember?

Sometimes remorse troubled you, or feelings of uneasiness tormented you. Your poor heart, without peace of quiet, bleeding at the center, could find no relief except at the feet of the crucifix and in the silence of prayer. Do you remember?

How many empty promises! How many broken engagements! Yet you were pure, my son, and destined to be mine. I knocked at the door of your heart and waited untiringly for the happy moment when I would call you mine! Do you remember?

All of a sudden the obstacles disappeared. You opened your wings and took your flight in the direction of this garden which had been prepared for you. You lit on the arms of the Cross

which was to sanctify you by its touch and preserve you beneath its blessed shade from the
snares of the enemy. Do you remember?

Who gave you strength to tear yourself from
the bosom of your family? Who detached your
heart from the vanities of this world, if not he
who from this consecrated Host whispers to you
in the innermost depth of your soul: Do you
remember?

Ah, yes, beloved son of my heart. Remember
always what you owe to your Jesus. Never forget
the benefits he has conferred on you and his special love for your soul.

Think often of the immensity of his love for
you, and become a saint. It is for this reason that
you have come here. Remember that it is not solitude that makes saints, but the desire. If you are
faithful, you will hardly ever find an hour where
you will not be able to make an act of self-denial.

Be of good courage then, and, in imitation of
Mary, remember the immense love of Jesus for
you. A remembrance of this will be worth a thousand graces.

Amen.

83. MY CONSOLATION

This is what I come to seek in your soul, my child: my consolation! No one can understand what my heart suffers and how great is my special love for crucified souls. Yet much will be required from him to whom much has been given, for I am very demanding in all that concerns a response to my graces.

I know how to withdraw and be silent when I find indifference in the hearts of creatures, when they neglect me and seek worldly comfort, when they make me second in their affection, when I am not the supreme object of their love.

Yet so great is my tenderness of heart for those who love the Cross, that putting aside the claims of justice, I condescend to the point of begging for their love.

What does this mean if not an inconceivable favoritism?

O my soul's beloved, I wish to be in this House the center of all hearts, the wellspring at which all thirst shall be quenched, the fire to give warmth to all, and the infinite charity which consumes them all.

Here indeed is my haven of rest, my Paradise on earth. I bear in my arms this small and humble community. I am the shepherd of this fold. I am the Master of this dovecote, the gardener of my lilies. I was crucified for all the souls here assembled. My heart is therefore their cradle, their resting place, their fortress and their life.

With my blood I feed the souls who live on the Cross. I make of them living crosses and beneath their shelter I take my rest, for in the world I see everywhere nothing but thorns.

It is I who have planted this cross in the garden of my Church, on which innumerable doves will make their nests and will lull me to sleep with their murmuring sighs of love. How, then, can I content myself, my beloved son, with parceled out fidelity and lukewarm love?

No, this small corner of the world so rich in privileges through my bounty, must burn with the same fire as the fire of my own heart, must live of its life, must develop itself in the silence of a love of expiation, must draw renewed strength from the consecrated Host, and form a chain of golden links which will reach to God's throne and bring down immense numbers of graces upon sinners.

I want purity to console my heart which has been torn apart by so many crimes.

I want victims who in union with me will call down graces on this corrupt world.

O beloved son of the Cross of my Heart, console it by your humility and by your hidden sacrifices, because I thirst for souls that are pure and crucified!

Be pure like unto the purity of the Eucharist itself. Love with the same love with which your Jesus has loved them.

Amen.

84. ALONE

This is the torment of torments, the solitude of the soul, this aching void, to find oneself alone and abandoned by God and man!

Alone! Who can understand the bitter feeling in that word except he that has tasted its bitterness? Nonetheless, God allows it. God sends those oceans of tribulation in which the soul is submerged and cleansed. He sends fire from heaven and even from hell itself with the loving motive of purifying it.

O Jesus, you who were forsaken by your disciples in the Garden of Olives, what shall I say to you today? That my heart has been plunged into profound affliction? Help me to keep the secret of the Cross so that I may give you the first fruits of my suffering. I wish to submit to the Divine will which makes me suffer. I pray only that you do not let me succumb to the temptations which assail me. Give me a lively faith to sustain me in the battle, a holy hope to preserve me from being discouraged, and a love above all loves which gives strength to fight valiantly amidst the storms which are bursting over me.

Where are you, Light of my darkness? I cannot see you!

Why do you not shine, Lord, like the stars you have created? Why do you leave my soul in this awful darkness? Where will I find consolation if I do not find you?

I am immersed in a flood of doubts, struggles, and sorrows. Save me, Lord, or I will perish. In you I have put all my hope and I will not be confounded forever.

But, O my good Jesus, what a miserable creature I am! When you console me, I am ready to offer myself as a victim. I ask you for crosses and abandon myself unreservedly to your will. But when you hide yourself ever so little, I immediately believe that you have forgotten me, that you have cast me aside, that you refuse your graces to me, and that the hour of mercy has passed for me.

How is it that I fail to realize that you were forsaken by your Heavenly Father, which did not stop you from being the Son of God and in no way diminished the infinite treasure of your merits or of my redemption.

How clearly this shows what I am! How weak, how worldly, how unfaithful and how ungrateful! How selfish is my love for you, and how faithless I am in giving back to you what I owe. I weaken and buckle under the weight of sorrow and contradiction, losing confidence, alas, in your mercy and in your loving presence. I am nothing but dust, weakness, sloth, misery. No wonder that I act this way.

O my Jesus, pardon me and console me in my trouble and desolation, by the light of your grace.

I do not ask you today not to forsake me, but only to strengthen my faith so that I do not separate myself from you, nor seek consolation from anywhere but from you. Humiliate me, but give me strength and courage to suffer unto death.

Give me strength, Lord, to struggle and to conquer. I beg it of you in memory of your abandonment by your disciples at the time of the Passion.

O, that I could renounce all consolation for love of you! My Jesus, give me the desire not even to detach myself from this Cross, and to be happy in the midst of these interior torments. Expand my heart so that you can pour more bitterness into it so that I may comprehend and love the Cross for the love of Jesus.

Alone, alone, alone! Such was your lot, O my Mother, during many long years after the death of Jesus. Ah, I beg you, by that terrible trial which you underwent with such admirable resignation, come to my assistance when Jesus conceals himself and leaves my soul apparently in the most cruel abandonment!

Amen.

85. «I CAME SO YOU COULD HAVE LIFE»

I feel that you have given me that life, my good Jesus. You give it to me again each day in the Sacrament of the Holy Eucharist.

Bread of Life! That is your real name, my Jesus. You took it one day when you said: «I am the Bread of Life» (John 6, 35). And I have that life in me for my happiness, since I receive you every morning into my heart. The remembrance of it during the day is my food and my strength.

— But how can that life be preserved, O Jesus, God of my soul?

— By dwelling in me. For if you dwell in me, I will dwell in you. Just as the vine branches cannot bear fruit if they are not united to the stalk, so also you can do nothing if you are not united to me.

— Our union must, then, be as close as that of the branch and the trunk of the tree: union of Life, my Treasure, my Jesus, my Life!

I wish to feed on your Divine Blood which washes away our sins. I wish to make my dwelling in the inmost recesses of your Heart where alone all real treasures are to be found.

I will not ask you, like David, to sprinkle me with hyssop, but with St. Peter I will ask you to wash my head, my hands and my feet in that Sacred Blood, so that I may become spotless and pure.

O Jesus, my only Love, who desires in the Sacrament of your Love to give me life, who preferred to lose all your Blood on the Cross so that my soul would not be lost, what return can I make to you for such love?

Your heart was resolved to separate itself from the soul which gave it life, and you will not, O my God, separate yourself from me who gave you death. Can one conceive a greater act of mercy?

You wish to be here, my Jesus, close to me, to speak to me, to listen to me, to answer me and to give me life. What stops me, Lord, from taking in this real life?

What stops me is that I live in myself and not in you. This is the contrary of what you do, because in your Heart sinners live and therefore, I, whom you love live there also. O my Jesus, who is it that deceives me and who is it that separates me from you? Who blinds me when I look at anything else but you? How long will I be borne down with this weight of misery, and when will there be nothing to stop me from living entirely in you?

If in your Heart I find a fire to consume me and to transform me, how can I suffer the icy coldness of my heart which kills me, and not throw myself at once into your arms, Lord, you who came to give me life?

O my hope and my only good! O my real life! O Jesus, more intimate to me than the most intimate recesses of my heart! I will say to you with St. Augustine: «unite me to yourself without intermediaries!» O life, without which I die, take away from me all life that is not yours, O Life of my life!

O Mary, you came into the world so Jesus should have life . . . you are the Mother of Life! Obtain for us, we humbly beg you, that our lives may be always a reflection of yours and of the life of Jesus.

Amen.

86. TO LOVE IS TO BE PURE

A pure soul resembles the most beautiful rose, and the three Divine Persons come down from Heaven to breathe its perfume.

There is nothing more beautiful than a pure soul! If we understood this, we would never soil the whiteness of our own!

A pure soul is detached from all material and earthly things. It forgets itself, for purity and humility always go together.

O my Jesus, who is Purity itself, O blood-stained Lily, immaculate flower of the Holy Eucharist, give me an immensity of love with which to love you, for in loving you I cannot offend you nor tarnish my soul. Give me love, O my Life, for love has the nature of fire, which is the most active and effective element. Give me that consuming fire which will destroy in my soul all its weaknesses, that invincible and ardent fire which will devour all my sins.

I want to have a love so pure, my Jesus, that it will be, as it were, a live coal ignited in the brasier of your Heart, that Heart all inflamed and burning with unequaled ardor, purifying all it touches and destroying our slightest imperfections.

I am burning with an ardent desire to be consumed in the furnace of your Heart, the origin and source of all Purity.

What keeps me, O Jesus, from losing myself in this furnace of love? My weaknesses and imperfections are the stumbling block. I am bereft of virtues, being overcome at every step by temptations, lukewarm and without fervor, without a lively desire to please you, without solicitude for serving you. I often see myself far from your arms, far from you, my only real life. When I see this, I cannot restrain my tears.

I realize what a short time I have to gain heaven, and how thoughtlessly I waste it in the pursuit of earthly things.

O my Jesus, infinite goodness and mercy, soul of my soul, what do I deserve but that you should deprive me of your tenderness? Give me tears of blood that I may weep for my ingratitude. Grant me also your pardon and your love, to give me back my baptismal innocence.

Is it not true that you will forget my past? Is it not true that you will give me today a spark of that celestial fire? O yes, my love, my heaven, my Jesus! Make me from now on think only of you and always forget myself.

What is worth desiring but you? What can be lacking to me if you give me yourself? O, how truly lost is that part of my life which I have lived without loving you!

Lord, open the springs of your Heart, that I may drink love and purity to the point of satiation! My most ardent desire is to be pure, to love you, to love you like Mary, to love you unto death.

Amen.

87. I AM A BIRD OF PASSAGE

Yes, my God, I am passing through, a wanderer and an exile on this earth, for my dwelling place is not here. Never will my heart have perfect peace until it reaches its Heavenly Home.

This life is not life, for Jesus is Life. He alone is life, and that is the life to which I must aspire, a life of purity and sanctity. O Jesus, my Life! When shall I die to myself so that I may possess You? I call You, O Jesus, from the depths of my soul, of my heart, for he who loves not lives not! Why wander about and seek happiness in so many created objects?

Love Jesus, the source of all good, in whom all goodness is contained. Love Him Who is life and in whom are enclosed all lives! You live in the flesh, and you aspire to a spiritual life! Mortify your flesh, and your soul will lift itself up to Jesus. O yes, my beloved, I wish to bid farewell to all but you, to all that does not lead to you. I wish to renounce myself, to die by inches every day, so that the happy day may arrive when I shall live no more, but you shall live in me . . . a day when I shall have no other life but yours!

How joyous is the thought that I am only passing through the world and that my way, the way that leads to Heaven, is the way of the Cross and the way of humiliations.

This way is our way, and we shall meet God in it only if we have purity of soul. Through sacrifice of ourselves we shall possess Him. God is not to be sought among the roses: Enter into the thorny bushes, like Moses, till you are covered with blood, and you will find Him.

What importance could all the thorns of life have if we can meet Jesus and possess Him!

O my Jesus, here present before me, Life of my life, make me to feel and understand these great truths, here, at your feet. Show me how to renounce myself, to be less every day, and how to detach my heart from everything on earth.

Teach me in loving to die, because love insists on different sorts of deaths, which I am ready to suffer at your feet.

I wish to die, my Jesus, during my life, that I may live eternally after my death.

O, that my eyes, Lord, be constantly turned toward heaven; that the ears of my soul may always hear the cry: «you are only passing» that it may detach me from all things here below, that my desires may be the same as yours. O Jesus and that I may nevermore think about myself except to renounce myself in imitation of Mary, my mother, Queen of Martyrs!

Amen.

88. «FOLLOW ME»

— While walking one day on the shores of the Lake of Galilee, I met Peter and Andrew, two souls whom I desired to attach to me forever. I said to them: «Follow me.» or what is the same thing, «Walk in my footsteps». More or less, this meant calling them to the Cross!

Those two generous souls followed me without a moment's hesitation, full of gratitude, and, true to the grace of their vocation, accompanied me, imitated me, loved me with all their strength. Both of them, after having suffered much for me, died on the Cross. That was their reward; to live with a thousand crosses, which they embraced and caressed and pressed to their noble hearts and then to die, in the sweet, friendly and gentle arms of that cross which was chosen for my elect!

To accompany me, to imitate me, to love me, those three things make souls happy in this life and prepare them for a holy death on the Cross.

Do you perhaps not know that it is but one step from the Cross to Heaven? What matters, then, a whole life of suffering with such a happy reward at the end! O my son, I took on myself all the rigors of the Cross; and ever since that day this sacred wood has offered nothing else but sweetness and delights to those souls who attached themselves to its embraces.

Do you remember that one day I brought my lips to your ear and said to you: «My son, you wander through the world like a dove without a nest . . . will you come to dwell in my Heart?» Come near to me and listen to its beatings:

O, how it beats for love of you! Follow me; you are not made for the world. I have loved you with an everlasting love. You have cost me streams of blood: you are mine; but will you be mine for ever? Will you come with me, and fade away like a flower beneath the burning heat of the Tabernacle? Will you come and be nailed to my own Cross, with the three precious nails of poverty, chastity, and obedience?

Never will you forget, son of the Cross and of Mary, that happy moment when I spoke to you of making you mine! What compliance! Never will you appreciate it enough!

You heard me and you broke with the world and its affections. Like those blessed apostles, you followed me, and here you are and here am I. Speak to me, then, of your love, and slowly recount to me your sorrows. A thousand times a day, my son, you should exclaim: «My beloved is mine and I am his». Weep over the ingratitude of man: for that is why you followed Me. Love with all your heart the follies of the Cross, and sacrifice yourself for the ungrateful. Think of me for those who do not think of me, and follow me to the highest point of Calvary. My Cross with open arms awaits you: My Cross and My glory, and with the Cross, your Jesus, the chosen of your heart, your consolation in your exile, your Joy, your Comfort, and your All.

Amen.

89. MY TURN HAS AT LAST ARRIVED!

Yes, my Jesus, my turn has arrived at last, the moment of drawing close to you for which I have been sighing for so long has at last arrived!

I come to tell you that I am full of sorrow, because I do not know how to love you more, and that I can find no perfect way of responding to your love.

I wish to tell you what a miserable wretch I am for not being able to put a guard on my senses as well as on my imagination and my memory. I wish to confide to you that I am displeased if others do not yield to my whims, that I am pained if I do not get what I want . . . that I am overly preoccupied with the things of this world, that I seek them with avidity and lose them with sorrow, and that you, alas, are not the sole and unique object of my love.

Can there be a greater sorrow, O love of all loves? Where are you, that you want to make me profit by so many graces and pardon me for so many weaknesses? How can I lose sight of you, Lord, and feel an icy chilliness in my heart when I ought to be burning by being in contact with you?

«Great graces, said St. Teresa, are only given to enable us to soar to the greatest heights, or, if they are abused, to precipitate us into the depths of hell». How then can I do anything else but fear, Lord? I have at my disposal so many ways of becoming a saint, and yet I am so cold, so miserable, so sinful, so vile.

In spite of all, my Jesus, I wish to love you without measure, and to sacrifice myself unceasingly.

Love! Enchanting, celestial, Divine word, which smells like Jesus, as a lily covered with blood . . . Happy would he be, O Jesus, who could live in you forever!

O Jesus, here present in the Holy Eucharist, during these precious moments of intimate confidences and ardent prayers, I beg you to make me charitable!

I wish to love you with a supernatural love, with a sovereign, constant, universal, emotional, practical, respectful and familiar love, a love of union with you most pure and most self-denying. In this way I wish to love you. Yet even if my love possessed these qualities, still my heart would not be content, but would wish to be still more purified, more transparent and luminous, in order to please you.

See, dearest Lord, you who hear me. I would have for you a love above all loves, greater than the love of the very seraphim, deeper than the ocean, more vast than the horizon, purer than all purity! To love you, I would have for you a love so special that it should identify my soul with yours, and be capable of melting my heart and burning it in your honor, so as to reduce it to ashes.

O my Jesus, why do you not give me your own heart with which to love you? O, when shall I see myself absorbed and consumed in you, O Celestial Fire, so pure and so sweet?

Chastise me, crush me, crucify me, for from this very moment I renounce everything in order to love you alone. Teach me to suffer without offending you, and to despise everything which is not you, my Jesus!

Teach me to suffer for you, and grant that my only sorrow may be to lose you and my only joy to love you.

Mary had no other joy in this world but to love you and to suffer with you for the same cause. That is what we, your poor children, desire . . . Ah yes, yes, my beloved Jesus!

Amen.

90.«AWAY WITH HIM! . . . CRUCIFY HIM!»

Alas, such is my cry, my beloved Lord, when I fail to obey the rules of my order, when I refuse to make some sacrifice, when I turn a deaf ear to your inspirations, in short, when I seek myself and close the doors of my heart against you.

«What harm have I done to you, my son?» you seem to ask me. Alas, how often, O my God, have I not said to myself, «I have no other king but Caesar», that is to say, my pleasures and my whims. As for you, Lord, withdraw from me, for you are an obstacle to my vanity, to my pride, and you prevent me from being glorified with the incense I wish to offer to myself.

O Jesus, my beloved Lord, who hears me. Here at your feet, let me ponder the sensations of your heart when you watch the behavior of your ungrateful creature. O my good Master, show me your heart torn in pieces for me by thorns, so that I may die of shame!

Is it I who stand far off and cry aloud for your death? Is it I who wish you to be removed from my gaze, you who are my Light? Is it I who make you suffer, when it is I who ought to make myself suffer for you? My Jesus, forgive me my innumerable sins and my continual lack of delicacy towards you. Never let me separate myself from you, nor allow yourself to be separated from me. Let those who hate you fail to see you. But I who love you, Lord, wish to drink of the life of your eyes, of the warmth of your heart. Come to me from now on, for I wish to be altogether yours, to adore you and sacrifice myself on the reverse side of your Cross, weeping over my infidelities and my weaknesses. Your sorrows shall be my strength, and your presence my life. There shall be no more delays in executing your wishes! You shall be my King, O Jesus, full of glory! Happy is he who would never lose sight of you and would carry your image graven in his heart!

Alas, my Love, when shall I loathe myself enough? . . . but I confess my weakness: every day I offer myself to you and place myself in your hands. I wish to imitate you, Jesus, but when the opportunity presents itself I no longer follow your inspirations, but allow myself to give away to my whims and evil inclinations. O my Lord, I attach myself here today to you who are all mercy and love! Forget my sins, and let your Love triumph in me. May you cry out, Lord, to the angels and to men: «Crucify him!» and then sustain me with your Divine Love!

Do not spurn me, Jesus, as I, miserable wretch, spurn you. O, most terrible were those hours in which I preferred the world and its comforts to the Cross! From now on make my happiness consist in humiliations and sorrows. In this way will you show your Power in drawing me to yourself and keeping me in your service for love of you.

I do not wish to remember the innumerable circumstances in which I spurned you and preferred myself to you, when I whispered to myself, «Let him be crucified». I will throw a veil over my past. Throw it yourself, Lord, and forget it and forgive me.

O Holy Virgin, ask the grace for me that the Cross may not leave my dwelling, nor its light my soul! By your intercession let me have the merit to be among the number of the crucified, so that I may be numbered one day among the glorified!

Amen.

91. I WISH TO DIE

O yes, I wish to die in order to obtain true life; to die at every step, to die unceasingly to myself in order to lead a spiritual life and to be able to exclaim, after a complete transformation, «to me, to live is Christ and to die is gain».

I wish to succeed in arriving at this transformation by a constant renunciation of my will, by means of that death which gives life, by that moral and spiritual death of self-denial for love of you.

How beautiful is that death which love always seeks: an active death which gradually deprives the old Adam of his life.

But to die once is not enough: this death must be renewed unceasingly: and every day one must begin to die again and never tire of doing so, so as to be born to another life, to put on another nature until one is able to say: «I live not, no, I am dead; it is Jesus, Jesus so sweet, so patient, Jesus crucified, Jesus humble and charitable, who lives in me. He alone remains in my soul. As for me, I have disappeared forever. My whims and my selfishness will also disappear, and Jesus alone shall remain the King of my soul».

O my Jesus, who is now listening to me, if I might want to return to my former life, do not let that happen. I promise you to master my passions and to remain ever at the feet of all others in the dust of my nothingness.

He who dies no longer has a will: he who dies has lost his liberty; he can be taken up or down, pulled about in all directions, without showing the least sign of pain, or uttering the slightest complaint.

What is a dead body fit for? To be buried, to be shunned, to be held in abhorrence, and not to be kept among the living.

O my God, will my pride ever place itself on the level of this dead body? Will it ever desire to be an object of loathing to all men?

Of myself I can do nothing, but if you, O my Jesus, my life, help me to die in this way, I shall rise again to the Divine life which you require of me, by triumphing over my weaknesses and my miseries.

O Holy Spirit, who is my strength! O true lover of my soul, help me also so to die in this life, that I may rise again to the life of grace.

O Jesus, all goodness and tenderness! O my love, my glory, and the consolation of my heart, be you yourself my life!

Let others seek what they will; as for me nothing pleases me, nothing satisfies me, but to live in your Life. O my God, Heart of my heart, my only hope and salvation! May the ardent flame of your Divine eyes give me death, and may the burning fire of your Heart consume me, so I may die of love, and that my death may resemble that of Mary, my most holy Mother!

Amen.

92. «THEY WHO SEEK ME EARLY, SHALL FIND ME»

These are the words of Jesus and they are always fulfilled.

Mary Magdelene went very early to the sepulchre of Jesus: it was she who had the first news about him, and met him first after his resurrection!

The prayer said before dawn is so beautiful. «You can believe my experience», said St. John Chrysostom, «when I tell you that, even as the fire purifies the iron of all rust, much more does night prayer purify the soul and cleanse it of its sins».

The bare earth was the bed of Jesus . . . his Head rested on a stone, with his Eyes fixed on Heaven during the silence of the night. What sighs escaped from that Heart burning with love! What tears coursed down those Divine cheeks, while he was imploring his Father to pardon our sins!

Jesus passed the whole night in prayer, in order to teach us to pray during that time. Indeed, just as the flowers that have been parched by the heat of the sun during the day, are refreshed by the coolness of the night, and receive the gentle dew from heaven, so also the soul, worn out and crushed by the struggles of the day, is refreshed by the dew of grace.

Who is there, my Jesus, who will not rise at dawn in order to meet you? . . . But these words also possess a figurative sense.

Happy are they who from their youth have consecrated themselves to you, O Jesus, and have given you their whole heart! «It is good for a man when he has adhered to his God from his youth».

A thousand times blessed are they who have given themselves to your service forever, before being contaminated by the poisoned shafts of the world, the flesh, and the devil!

Happy are they, O Jesus, who have come here to open their souls for the first time, like the humblest flowers at the foot of your tabernacle, beneath the gentle rays of your Love!

Happy lilies opening their petals to Heaven in this garden of the Bridegroom, in the midst of those precious flowers, whose perfumes are gathered by the angels!

There is another reason for being up early sometimes. It is to find out as soon as possible what the Will of God is and then do it. What does it matter that Jesus sends us the Cross in a thousand different shapes, since we are always sure to find him close to it!

In this way one practices the beautiful virtue of generosity, which divines the smallest wishes of Jesus, and which tears out from his Head the cruel thorns in order to implant them on our own heads.

It is in this way that one wins the friendship of Jesus. It is in this way that one meets him, in going to meet every sacrifice for love of him. Who would act otherwise in this House of the Cross? Who will remain slothful in this House of Sorrows?

O Jesus, you who hear me in your adorable Sacrament! Give me that dedication of being always ready at break of day to sacrifice myself for you, and to meet you at the hour of my meditation!

O Mary, you went out at dawn, on the day of the death of your Jesus, and you met him going to the sacrifice, to the Cross. Teach my soul to be the first to follow Jesus to Calvary, and to sacrifice myself with him!

Amen.

93. «WHO CAN EVER SEPARATE ME FROM HIM?»

No one! Nothing, my Jesus; neither death, nor life, nor trials, nor joys, nor health, nor sickness, nor crosses, nor martyrdom, nor torments, nor all tortures combined . . . these will rather be the sacred bonds which will bind me still more closely to you and to your most loving Heart.

One thing only could separate me from you, O my only good, O infinite gentleness, O incomparable beauty, and that is sin! That monster alone could put a barrier between you and me. But you will not allow it, my gentle immaculate Lamb, and I beg you to let me die rather than offend you.

I tremble at the mere thought that it may be possible for me to be separated from you, O Life of my soul! For if you forsake me, I am bereft of all light and warmth, of grace and of Heaven!

Punish me, Lord, in whatever way you wish: crucify me and do with me what you wish, but attach me to your Heart with the same crown of thorns that bound you. Nail me to your Cross with the same nails that crucified you. I shall be happy provided I do not offend you, and that I be never more separated from you.

Grant me the grace, Lord, to repel with horror all that could separate me from you. Make me show the greatest love and affection for all that can draw me nearer to you.

May all my happiness consist in suffering for you.

O my good Jesus, crucify me with yourself on the Cross! Nail it to my body and my heart close to yours. In the Cross are health, strength, safety, life! I wish to live on the sap of that Divine tree, to retire beneath the shade of its branches and to feed on its heavenly fruit . . . In this way it will not be possible for me to be separated from You, for the Cross is the glorious companion of the elect.

O Jesus, God and Spouse of my soul, it is not without reason that the Cross inspires me with love, and that I feel a violent desire to throw myself into its arms, to carry it on my shoulders, and to press it to my heart. The Cross was the treasure house of your riches, the confidante of your secrets, the triumph of your victories.

The Cross received into its arms your body and your loving Heart, and one day you promised that all those who should receive its imprint would be recognized as being yours, and that those whom the Cross accompanied should always be protected by you. How, then, shall I not love it with enthusiasm, since it is the peculiar sign of those whom you love? How, then, shall I not love all kinds of crosses? How shall I not burn with a desire to suffer for my Lord? How shall I not consider as lost the hour that I pass without suffering? I wish, my Jesus, to see myself, ah yes, as you did see yourself . . . nailed on a cross. If you have suffered for me, how should I not wish to suffer for you?

When shall I consider it a consolation, not to be consoled in imitation of you? O God of Love! O Love of God! I only really love you when I sacrifice myself for you, and render you love for love.

O Jesus, O my love, give me your Cross or let me die! Make me die, by the fire of your love: may I expire this very moment, if I may not spend my whole life in suffering for you!

I know that you will not fail me. I know that you will never forsake one who has crucified himself for love of you. I know that you love most tenderly those whom you nail to the Cross. Love me, my beloved Jesus, love me and crucify me, as you crucified your most Holy Mother wishing that she should resemble you more!

Amen.

94. «MY YOKE IS SWEET AND MY BURDEN LIGHT»

My soul has learned it by experience, O Jesus of the Eucharist! The more the weight of suffering tries to crush me, the more I feel in my inmost soul a Divine strength which sustains me, something supernatural which helps me to carry the Cross, and makes it light and easy to bear.

The yoke requires two bearers . . . and who then is that other bearer, Lord, but you yourself, who softens and sweetens all that suffering? You are right, indeed, to assure us that your burden is light, for you carry the heaviest part of it. In this way you deprive the Cross of its bitterness, so that the heart that loves you cannot do without you.

It is quite true! it is very sweet to suffer, when one has Jesus in one's heart! Pain is so agreeable when one suffers only for love!

If trials and contradictions are the road which leads us to Calvary, the Cross, which is planted at the summit of this holy mountain, is in truth the gate of Heaven.

The sufferings of this world pass away, but the torments of the other life are eternal. What does it matter, then, if life is full of trials and anguish, if this life is the river which will one day bear us on its bosom into the Ocean of Heaven? Let us carry the Cross joyfully, enthusiastically, fervently; for to live on the Cross is to live on love.

O my good Jesus who hears me now, give me the grace to follow this way of voluntary immolation, so that my life may be consumed in your honor.

Like St. Francis Xavier, after a life of troubles, trials and contradictions, I would sigh and cry out in the midst of all these crosses. «Amplius, Domine!» Still more Lord, even if our poor nature resists! It does not matter, for although I suffer and weep, your yoke shall always be sweet and your burden light, on account of my ardent love for you.

I know that peace does not consist in being without temptations, but rather in never offending you, and that is what I desire and wish with all my soul: never to offend you, and to die rather than to sin or fail to be obedient to my superiors, or to cause you sorrow!

I wish to glory in being forgotten and despised. I wish to rejoice in the folly of the Cross, and to long for humiliations and self-denial.

I thirst to go down further, and this thirst cries aloud in my soul for more humility, more obscurity and voluntary annihilation.

I desire most ardently, my Jesus, to be a victim in union with you, and for a victim in adoration, there exist most profound and unfathomable depths, to which he must descend.

I fear neither suffering nor humiliation, Lord, since I know that you help me, and that the Cross is light and your yoke is sweet: with this thought ever present before me and with the assistance of your grace which will not fail me, I am ready to climb every Mount Calvary, life being too short to allow me to suffer for you as much as I would!

O Jesus, all sweetness, mercy and love! O Spouse of my soul and splendor of eternal glory, when will the day arrive when I shall forget myself and be entirely occupied in carrying the Cross, that sweetest of all burdens, which is rendered light by love!

O Mary, obtain, I beseech you, that the Cross, this yoke of Jesus, may always be sweet for us and that his burden may always be light!

Amen.

95. «BUT JESUS WAS SILENT»

What a model of silence and humility is Jesus in the Pretorium before Pilate, in the Palace of Herod . . . and now in the Holy Eucharist!

Jesus is silent before the insults, the mocking, and the bitter sarcasm of his enemies. Silent in the presence of ingratitude, neglect and scorn, alas, of his friends, of those who called themselves his by so many titles!

Poor Jesus! With what delicacy he conceals my sins, effaces them with his Blood and purifies them by his innocence . . . he hides them by his goodness and pardons them with his love!

How often, after having wounded his Heart by my pride, my impatience, and my want of generosity, have I not cast myself at his feet, and instead of reproaching me for my weakness, Jesus was silent, and smiled. I seemed to hear him saying in the depths of my soul: «Fear not, for the measure of my love is beyond all measure». How eloquent are these periods of silence of Jesus! They captivate the heart, penetrate it with humility, and fill it with boundless love!

Could I perhaps imitate this silence? Could I hold my peace at least when duty obliges me to do so? Could I shut my lips concerning the faults of my neighbors? Do I take care not to excuse myself, when I am reproved for some fault? O my Jesus, how far I am from resembling you! You hide my weaknesses, and I publicize those of my neighbors! You pardon me in your goodness, and I cannot forget an injury!

You are silent under a storm of opprobium and ingratitude; and I utter bitter complaints about trifles. This comes from the fact that my humility is only in my lips, and that pride is deeply rooted in my inmost heart.

Dissipation and pride are the sources of my sinning against silence, my Jesus. If I meditated on your Passion, if I lived that interior life, which unites us so firmly to you, I should learn from your Divine lips how to keep silent when my feelings are wounded by offensive words, how to keep the Secret of the Cross and never to utter a complaint and to always be gentle and patient, loving and charitable.

O my Jesus, who is now listening to me, lend me today those Divine lips which uttered only words of tenderness and love! Grant me this blessed gift of silence which sweetens all things and raises up the soul to union with God! Put a stop to the tumult to which my own passions give birth, and may my tongue from now on be occupied only in praising you, that You may be loved by everyone.

Enough and more than enough of all these sins. Help me to acquire in all their perfection, the virtues of gentleness, kindness and charity. You shall be the honey to sweeten all my bitterness, and through you, O Mary, may there be brought into my relations with my brethren that tenderness and delicate tact which may do good to their souls.

O, had I only kept my peace on many different occasions! My soul would be filled with your light, enriched with your graces, transformed into you, inflamed with Divine love, pure and free from all the faults which I have committed owing to my having failed to keep my peace!

Amen.

96. «THE KINGDOM OF HEAVEN SUFFERS VIOLENCE»

True it is, my Jesus, and only those shall enter into this Kingdom, who, doing violence to themselves, triumph over the world, the devil and themselves.

The Cross is the weapon which on the field of battle shall give us the victory. Without the Cross we should die with shame after being defeated. We should be as dead branches separated from the trunk and only fit for the fire.

Self-denial and renunciation! In these two words are to be found the secret of victory, the hidden spring which will give the necessary incentive to raise us up to heaven. The way which leads to eternal glory is narrow, and only the brave pass over it with a smile on their lips. But once more, what are thorns to one who wishes to be crucified for his Beloved One?

I am never better, said St. Francis de Sales than when I am not well. I come to ask you today, O Jesus, for a similar frame of mind. Give me that courage which is the exclusive product of love.

I wish to take Heaven by force, even at the cost of my heart's blood, even in leaving fragments of my flesh on the thorns on the way. I wish to do violence to myself and to live as a martyr, so as not to die eternally. «Cut, burn, crush», I shall say again with St. Augustine, «on condition that in the other life you shall never separate me from yourself».

O my Jesus, put my soul into the crucible, and cleanse and purify it of its dross. I want to be happy throughout all eternity, but that I cannot be without grace and without suffering. It is not possible to be really happy in this world without destroying in oneself that which constitutes natural happiness! . . . O my beloved Jesus, if heaven is the reward of mortifications and of the Cross, that is to say of those who do violence to themselves, I will from this very moment ascend to Mount Calvary and never come down from it again. I wish to belong to you at all costs and forever, and I know that the more I shall be crucified, the more I shall be yours. I will therefore no more complain of being forsaken by God and men. At every opportunity I will tear myself away from myself and from all I love, and always immolate my heart in your honor.

When temptations assail me, when there seems to be no end to my soul's darkness, when nobody understands me, and storms rage in my soul, I will do violence to myself, and I will hope against all hope without ever faltering on the way of the Cross.

I will struggle with the help of your grace after each storm, and never weary in doing so. Ever invincible, with Mary for my guide, I shall take by force the eternal kingdom. I shall enter therein, as it is said those souls enter who have loved and borne the Cross like a Queen entering into her palace!

Amen.

97. WHAT DO YOU DESIRE?

O my Jesus, my Glory, my Happiness! Speak to my heart which is thirsting to please you. Speak to it and give me the intelligence to understand and practice what you will ask of it.

What do you want, my Jesus, what do you want?

— I desire your perfection, my child, beloved son of my soul. I want you to become a saint. Be of good courage then. Open your wings and fly among the places which I shall show you. Fear nothing, for aided by me and by your heavenly Mother, you can do all things.

I desire of you, O my son of the Cross, a universal detachment from all human things: from affection, persons and riches. You must tear your heart in pieces as to what concerns friendships, comforts, the various attachments of the mind, the demands of the body. You must crucify your flesh for my honor and my love.

The vow of poverty will have detached you from material things, but this detachment must also be observed, in accordance with my will, in spiritual things.

You must entirely destroy your judgements, opinions, and ways of looking at things.

Cut off one by one all the ties which bind you to earth, and, without pity, break off any friendship which could in any way estrange you from my affection.

Never deliberately consent to seek yourself, but indignantly chase away all self-satisfaction. Do not endeavor in a more or less hypocritical way, to earn the applause of your neighbors. Do not desire the good opinion of others, nor to be looked upon as one worthy of attracting attention.

Do not think yourself capable of doing anything by yourself, except to do evil, and to damn yourself.

As soon as you think that you perceive some good in yourself, turn away and humble yourself profoundly. Remember what you are and the innumerable weaknesses which, as I have shown you a thousand times, exist in the depths of your soul. Let temptations pass without touching you, and remain hidden in your seclusion and in your nothingness.

And finally, never do anything with the deliberate intention of seeking your own satisfaction! O, how many similar faults are committed, and what vast horizons of perfection will present themselves to your view in the practice of these virtues, if you carefully guard yourself against what I have told you. This is an excellent way of destroying the old Adam and of enriching, with the life of God himself, the soul which has reached these heights.

That is real self-denial and an unceasing death; the soul that arrives at this degree of perfection, lives only by mortifications and the Cross.

Strive to reach these heights, if you want to please me and really sanctify yourself.

Onward, my son, onward! Love will give you strength. You must die yourself in order to attain the real life. You must begin this transformation in me, and it will only be complete when you have killed your own heart.

To do this is to deny yourself, to give up all and to follow me, for this is love.

Amen.

98. «BE PERFECT AS MY HEAVENLY FATHER ALSO IS PERFECT»

Perfection, my son, consists in loving God with humility and above all things, and one's neighbor as oneself, for the love of God.

This love must be accompanied by humility.

But how does one love God with humility?

— By the total submission of one's judgement to all the dispositions of Divine Providence.

— By offering oneself as a victim, as incense destined to be burnt for the greater glory of my Father, without anyone knowing it and without even thinking that I shall be grateful for it. In a word, by offering oneself for all sorts of immolation with a purely disinterested love.

— By receiving with excessive gratitude the graces, small or great, with which I favor souls, and by being utterly confounded at my benevolence.

— By rejoicing to imitate me, by enduring the contempt of all men.

— By taking me for a model crucified; by copying me in my Passion out of love. By shunning all honors.

— By returning the graces received into my hands with gratitude, by means of perfect spiritual poverty, and believing yourself unworthy of having received them.

— By loving me because I am he who is . . . without interest, without being ambitious of reward, believing that one is not worthy to love me.

— By never failing to trust in my goodness and in my merits . . . never under any circumstances.

— By considering oneself with all one's heart and at all times, unworthy to be in my service and exceedingly happy to be even tolerated there.

— By ever wishing to hide yourself so that I may shine, to disappear that I may appear, to cease to exist that I alone may reign.

— By receiving and accepting with the same gratitude pleasant and painful things, desolation or consolation, placing your only joy in my present or future will, and to do this under the impulse of a love that wishes to renounce itself.

Do you now understand what it is to love God with humility? It is the highest perfection, not impossible of attainment by the creature, when it comes by means of my grace.

What does it mean, then, to love men with humility?

We love men with humility, if we hide from them the sacrifices we offer or impose on ourselves for them, so that God alone is witness to them. It is in this way that you must love them, my son, by sacrificing yourself secretly for them. To give yourself to others in this way with the object of pleasing me, is also a proof of love for me, your Jesus, since I am the goal of this sublime act of charity whose value is enhanced by my imitation and my merits.

How many sacrifices have I not made for my guilty sons during my life, sacrifices which will only be known in the next world!

He who shall love me with this love of humility will give evident proof that this love is real, if he be not selfish, if he be ready to give willingly what he has received in sacrificing himself for others. The love of him in whose soul this tendency does not exist, is open to suspicion. That is to say, his love is neither very pure nor very fervent. For as love for me grows in a soul, so, also at the same time does the love for one's neighbor increase, as well as the ardent thirst to communicate graces which have been acquired by sacrifice.

Thus is it that we love God and our neighbor with humility; in this way we arrive at perfection; in this way we ascend to Heaven.

Mary, our model, loved God and men in this way, with humility . . . thus must we love, we, the beloved children of Jesus and Mary.

Amen.

99. THAT FLOWER!

O my Jesus! How envious I feel at the sight of that flower which I see every day close to your Tabernacle! I see it first in the bud, opening out little by little. I say to it: «You are growing and becoming beautiful, in order to be offered to Jesus in the Holy Eucharist, and to shed your petals slowly at his feet. Who would not wish to take your place? Who would not envy the same happiness? With tears in my eyes my heart envies your lot».

And when I gaze at that flower on your Altar, O Jesus, full of dew and loving confidence, I place upon it my fondest embraces and caresses, my loves and my sorrows, to be presented to you, O my beloved!

I shall shortly have to leave this chapel, my Jesus, in order to perform my daily duties, but that flower will remain before you, every hour, every instant, sacrificing to you its colors and its perfume, slowly dying in the warmth of your Altar.

O Jesus, my adorable Jesus, I wish I could be for you a little flower and not a big thorn!

See, Lord, how different are our two lives; that flower was pruned and grew up for your glory. And I? I was born and grew up for the world with its vanities, for myself and my comforts, to offend you a thousand times, and in withdrawing from you to run after worldly pleasures, and everything but you, Beloved of my soul!

That flower has kept itself immaculate. It will die in all its spotless purity on your Altar. It has kept for you the freshness of its bloom and its innocence . . . And I? That flower has not served the world for a single day . . . And I?

At times it is quite white as if to shame me. At others it is red, in order to show me that, since I am not pure, I must at least be on the Cross. It tells me to cleanse my soul and to present it as a little flower to the dew of grace, to the drops of your Blood, which will deposit in it the germ of all virtues.

O my beloved Jesus, let me remind you with emotion of all the favors you have granted to me, in spite of my unworthiness.

It is true, Lord, and I avow it with shame. I have given to the world the leaves, the bark, the exterior, but it is also true that you have closed my interior and that you have always drawn me to the foot of your Altar. You have surely kept what was yours: that sanctuary, that closed bud of my soul, which only opened out in response to the rays of the Divine sun!

«I want you for myself alone», you said to me one day when I was weeping over my ingratitude at your feet. «I will be yours», my soul answered you with ineffable joy.

And all friendships, all affections, and all loves, even the most holy, have never invaded this sanctuary in which you dwell. You triumphed on that day, O master of my being, my only Good, my Jesus! And since the day you won this ungrateful heart for yourself, I have become yours more and more. But I wish to be yours still more . . .

I wish to be a humble violet to live and die in your Heart of fire. I wish to be modest, humble, gentle, patient, to be entirely at the disposal of others, to allow myself to be contradicted, persecuted, without anybody knowing it, without anyone even suspecting my sacrifices.

I will hide, like the violet, from the gaze of men, and I will hide you, o my Jesus, in the midst of the misery and poverty of my heart.

Grant me, O my Jesus, to live and die close to you, like that little flower. Let us both be the victims of sinners, both glorifying the Eternal Father, both offering ourselves by the hands of Mary, without ever separating one from the other: our hearts, our souls and our lives, flowers of heaven, shedding the last drops of our blood out of love.

Amen.

100. TO BE A SAINT

This is my heart's desire, O my beloved Jesus! To be a saint in order to be yours: to renounce myself, forever die to myself to rise again with you.

But what is a saint, my adorable Jesus?

— To be a saint, my son, is to ascend a ladder of crosses without ever stopping, with a smile on the lips, with the love of humility in the heart.

A saint never loses sight of me, having the supernatural desire to glorify God in everything.

A saint sees unceasingly, with the eyes of the soul, his Jesus crucified; he imitates him in keeping immaculate the purity of his soul.

A saint judges all men charitably, performs all his duties with perfection, and forgets nothing but himself. He never complains if he is treated with discourtesy or disrespect since he believes himself to be utterly worthless.

To be a saint, is not only to do well the thousand and one ordinary actions of life, but to do them perfectly, with purity of intention, with diligence, and to perform in a supernatural spirit each of these actions for love in a spirit of immolation.

To be a saint, is to be an apostle in one's silence and in one's speech, by example and by the heroic practice of all the virtues. To be a saint is to rejoice in the midst of the greatest humiliations; to be fascinated by the sweet and delicate joys of the Cross, in abandonment, contempt, and obscurity, without any other witness but God alone.

To be a saint, is to sacrifice one's life blood drop by drop, in tearing out of the fibers of one's heart, one by one, all that is not purely for God.

To be a saint, is to be a real son of Mary, a perfect imitator of her hidden virtues.

To be a saint, is to let oneself be crucified by God and by man, gently, patiently and humbly, in silence, in a spirit of gratitude, in accepting everything that can make one suffer without ever losing peace of soul.

To be a saint, is to lead an interior life hidden in God, a life of union with him by means of unceasing prayer and meditation, and never, so to speak, letting a moment pass without practicing some virtue.

To be a saint, is to break with all that is natural: it is to have a heart totally abandoned to the Divine will. It is to choose always and in everything what will cause the greatest suffering: it is to love suffering, to desire it and to rejoice in it . . . all that solely for the love of God and of souls.

To be a saint, is to lead a life of voluntary self-effacement, ever more humble and obscure . . . it is to be transformed into me by humility, by love, by suffering and by pain.

If you want to be a saint, say from the depths of your soul, and put into practice this beautiful motto:

Nothing for nature, all for God!

God alone is the life of the saints . . .

Amen.

Sisters of the Cross
of the Sacred Heart of Jesus
1320 Maze Blvd.
Modesto, CA 95351
U.S.A.

Missionaries of the Holy Spirit
529 W.4th street
Oxnard, CA 93030
U.S.A.

Missionaries of the Holy Spirit
6450 Parkcrest St.
Long Beach, CA 90808
U.S.A.

Missionaries of the Holy Spirit
Parish of Saint Martha
6019 Stafford Ave.
Huntington Park, CA 90255
U.S.A.

Missionaries of the Holy Spirit
Our Lady of Guadalupe Parish
500 N. Juanita Ave.
Oxnard, CA 93030
U.S.A.

Missionaries of the Holy Spirit
2512 187th Pl. SE.
Bothell, WA 98012-6534
U.S.A.

Missionaries of the Holy Spirit
House of Studies
585 E. College St.
Mount Angel, OR 97362

Missionaries of the Holy Spirit
447 SE 3rd Ave
Hillsboro, OR 97123-4499
U.S.A.

To order additional copies of this book:

Please complete the form below and send for each copy

CMJ Marian Publishing
P.O. Box 661 • Oak Lawn, IL 60454
call 708-636-2995 or fax 708-636-2855
email jwby@aol.com
www.cmjbooks.com

Name _____

Address _____

City _____ State _____ Zip _____

Phone ( ) _____

		QUANTITY		SUBTOTAL
Before the Altar $ 12.00 each	x	_____	=	$ _____
Though I Walk Through the Valley				
$ 14.95 each	x	_____	=	$ _____
Crosses and Joys of Aging				
$ 12.95 each	x	_____	=	$ _____
The Grunt Padre (hardcover)				
$ 22.95 each	x	_____	=	$ _____
The Grunt Padre (softcover)				
$ 15.95 each	x	_____	=	$ _____
Radiating Christ $ 11.00 each	x	_____	=	$ _____
Becoming the Handmaid of the Lord				
$ 13.95 each	x	_____	=	$ _____
The Cheese Stands Alone				
$ 12.50 each	x	_____	=	$ _____
+ tax (for Illinois residents only)			=	$ _____
+ 15% for S & H			=	$ _____
TOTAL			=	$ _____

Check # _____ Visa MasterCard Exp Date ___ / ___ / ___

Card # _____

Signature